PRACTICAL INTERFAITH

How to Find Our Common Humanity as We Celebrate Diversity

REV. STEVEN GREENEBAUM

Walking Together, Finding the Way ®

SKYLIGHT PATHS®
PUBLISHING
Woodstock, Vermont

www.skylightpaths.com

Practical Interfaith:
How to Find Our Common Humanity as We Celebrate Diversity

2014 Quality Paperback Edition, First Printing
© 2014 by Steven Greenebaum

Library of Congress Cataloging-in-Publication Data
Greenebaum, Steven.
  Practical interfaith : how to find our common humanity as we celebrate diversity / Rev. Steven Greenebaum.
      pages cm
  Includes bibliographical references and index.
  ISBN 978-1-59473-569-1 (alk. paper) — ISBN 978-1-59473-590-5 (ebook : alk. paper)
1. Religions—Relations. 2. Religious pluralism. I. Title.
  BL410.G74 2014
  201'.5—dc23
                                    2014030558

10 9 8 7 6 5 4 3 2 1
Manufactured in United States of America
Cover Design: Jenny Buono
Interior Design: Tim Holtz

Walking Together, Finding the Way
Published by SkyLight Paths Publishing
A Division of LongHill Partners, Inc.
Sunset Farm Offices, Route 4, P.O. Box 237
Woodstock, VT 05091
Tel: (802) 457-4000 Fax: (802) 457-4004
www.skylightpaths.com

To all, throughout history, who put love and
compassion above doctrine and sect.

CONTENTS

PREFACE

It's news to no one that we live in a world in conflict. I must confess that it still amazes me how adept and creative we are at finding ways to divide ourselves into "us" and "them." If we ever find life in space, I have no doubt that there will immediately arise an Earth versus whomever drumbeat. Since we haven't, at least as yet, we must settle for somewhat less cosmic divisions. We have blocs of countries in constant tension if not at war with other blocs, as well as individual countries lining up against one another. Within countries we have gender divisions, age divisions, ethnic divisions, racial divisions, and territorial divisions, to name just a few. In the United States, as example, we take "pride" in our state, our city, and perhaps even our neighborhood. Some of us are actually willing to come to blows over our sports teams.

One of our most ancient and destructive divisions has to do with our spiritual paths. The truth of it is, we have been hating and slaughtering each other over differences about God (or no God) for millennia. In my first book, *The Interfaith Alternative*, I tried to chronicle the how and why of this.

When I wrote *The Interfaith Alternative*, I drew on a lifetime of experience. There were many a twist and turn, and more than a few surprises, in the evolution of my spiritual self as I struggled to understand and then to communicate Interfaith as a faith among our spiritual paths.

I prefer to use the term "spiritual path" rather than "religion," for the simple but important reason that many of our spiritual paths aren't religions. We'll look at this more deeply later in this book, but for now, consider that Humanism is a spiritual path but not a religion. Buddhism likewise is a spiritual path but not a religion. In *The Interfaith Alternative*, I looked at the poisonous paradigm of "right belief," the idea that there is one and only one right answer to the question of God. I then asked, Is there an

viii   Preface

alternative to this paradigm? And there is. There is an Interfaith alternative, grounded in a theology broad enough to include us all.

Also, while I have no hesitation referring to God, I will frequently speak of "the sacred." Why? I believe in God, but I know and respect that not all of us do. What we all hold in common, whether we believe in God or not, is a sense of the sacred—spiritual matters that we hold close, that can help guide us toward our shared goal of love, compassion, and community.

Christianity, Islam, Judaism, Buddhism, Humanism, Baha'ism, and countless other beautiful and profound spiritual paths can *all* lead us to the sacred. They can all be righteous paths. But they can also lead us astray— all of them. What Interfaith teaches us is that it is not the path we walk, but how we walk our path that counts.

And that's pretty much where *The Interfaith Alternative* ends. The book was intended to be, and I hope remains, a call for us to put aside our us-and-them outlook on our spiritual lives. When I self-identify by saying my faith is Interfaith and my spiritual path is Judaism, I am acknowledging not only that there are a multitude of spiritual paths that might be walked, but that they can also be good and profound paths. At the same moment I am saying that the path I happen to walk is Judaism—not because Judaism provides the one right path for the world, but because Judaism has, throughout my life, been the path that has been the most helpful to me in guiding me toward a life of love, compassion, and community. At the same moment I know and happily acknowledge that I have friends who walk the path of Christianity, Islam, Buddhism, Humanism, the Baha'i, and others, whose paths have helped guide them to lives of love, compassion, and community. The call of *The Interfaith Alternative* is to show that it's not only possible to put aside the one-size-fits-all or my-way-or-the-highway approach to our spiritual lives, but actually desirable. Just as important, we need not put aside or abandon our own spiritual paths in order to respect and honor the paths of others.

The response to the book has for the most part been hugely gratifying and positive. But in my travels and discussions, three questions in particular have been raised over and over again:

1. "Interfaith sounds wonderful," I'm told by many (but clearly not all, and I deeply respect that). "But do I have to leave my own spiritual path to join?"

2. "There aren't any Interfaith churches near me. How do we start one?"

3. "Interfaith sounds like a wonderful way to live, but how do we get there?"

These practical questions are the reason for this book, *Practical Interfaith*. *The Interfaith Alternative* was intended as a welcoming introduction to Interfaith as a faith. We examined the why of Interfaith and explored a theological framework for it. Here I want to continue the welcome, as we further explore and develop Interfaith as a faith, and then examine the exciting and important questions "What can I do?" and "How can I get involved?" A simple word of caution: This book is a deeply personal document that explores Interfaith as a faith, and how we can make it work. It is not intended as a comprehensive overview of interfaith relations.

One interesting thing that they don't think to teach you in seminary is how to start a new faith community. I've pretty much had to invent things as I go. As I write this, Living Interfaith Church is completing its fourth year. In hopes that you will not have to reinvent the wheel, I've tried to put down here some of what we've learned, what we as a new spiritual community based on Interfaith have learned—what has worked, and, quite frankly, what hasn't. The purpose of writing this is not to establish the one right way to form an Interfaith church. Rather, here is what we did (and it has very much been a "we" experience) and why and how it worked out. Hopefully, others will build on this start, for it is clearly only a start.

Also, while my hope is that at least most of the readers of this book will have read *The Interfaith Alternative* before exploring here, I realize that some—in fact, many—have not. So Part One, "The Call of Interfaith," is intended as a broadening review for those who have read *The Interfaith Alternative* and a rather condensed introduction to Interfaith for those who haven't.

I understand and respect that all of us will approach Interfaith and this book a little differently. Still, my hope is that you will feel inclined, perhaps having read the book once, to read it again as part of a group of three or four or more. Particularly with these readers in mind, each chapter concludes with a page titled, "A Bit Deeper: Questions for Discussion." Here you'll find some questions designed to help readers discuss and explore both the chapter they've been reading and the spiritual thoughts of fellow readers.

At the end of each section of the book are "Voices of Interfaith." I thought it would be of interest to hear a few voices other than mine! I asked members of Living Interfaith to share in a few paragraphs their spiritual journeys and how they ended up as members of the Living Interfaith Church. They have done so eloquently, and it is a pleasure to share their thoughts with you.

Part I

THE CALL OF INTERFAITH

1

INTERFAITH AS A FAITH

We live in hugely troubled times. Isn't it time for humanity to come together and embrace our spiritual diversity, rather than coming to blows over it? Isn't it time to recognize that all of our spiritual paths have called on us—begged us—to shelve our hate, to step outside of our divided worlds, and to come together in love, compassion, and community? Isn't it at long last time to unite in common purpose to address the problems that have plagued us separately for so very long? If so, just how might we manage this small miracle? One possible answer is Interfaith as a faith, a faith that calls us to embrace and celebrate our spiritual diversity.

I presented Interfaith as a faith in my first book, *The Interfaith Alternative*. After it was published, I went on a book tour and was told rather pointedly at more than one of my stops that if there is one thing humanity does *not* need it's another religion. Whether one agrees with that statement or not, what it told me was that there may be some confusion between "faith" and "religion." It is important to understand that Interfaith is not a new religion but, rather, a faith that may offer us a powerful and positive way to move forward.

So what's the difference?

Put simply, a religion is a systematized faith, rooted in culture. Every religion, like every language, has its own vocabulary and grammar. Indeed,

I think it is helpful to think of our varying religions as languages for speaking to and about God and the sacred. Some languages are similar to each other or even related to each other, while others are vastly different. This doesn't make one language right and another wrong. It means that differing languages have differing rules that make them unique and powerful modes of expression.

The Faith of Interfaith

Interfaith, as a faith, does not seek to create a new sacred language. Rather, it teaches that whatever our sacred language, it is what we *say* with it that is truly important. Just as we can write works of both profound beauty and vile pornography in any language, so we can live a life of justice and compassion or a life of arrogant small-mindedness walking any of our spiritual paths. This being the case, Interfaith tells us that what truly counts is not the religion we practice but how we practice our religion.

Interfaith also acknowledges that there is more to our spiritual selves than just our established religions. As already noted, Buddhism and Humanism are not considered religions. For this reason I prefer to refer to our "spiritual paths," rather than "religions." Our spiritual paths are the sacred beliefs—that may or may not include belief in the Divine—that inform the way we walk, structured or not, toward the universal goal of a meaningful and fulfilling life. Thus, while all religions are spiritual paths, not all spiritual paths are religions.

Interfaith, as a faith, teaches us that our spiritual paths are hugely important. The truth is that *none* of us would be who we are if we did not believe what we believe. Yet Interfaith embraces as a foundational article of our faith that there are many right paths to the sacred. As a beautiful Japanese folk saying puts it, "There are many roads to the top of Mount Fuji." So, to rephrase the point we made a few moments ago, it is not the spiritual path we walk, but how we walk our path that determines the kind of life we will lead.

More than that, Interfaith teaches that our spiritual paths should not be seen as isolated. Rather, our differing paths are connected by our common humanity. As the English poet John Donne might have put it, no spiritual path is an island, entire of itself. Each path is a piece of the continent, a part of the whole.

The Dilemma of Right Belief

If each path is a part of the whole, what then do we do about our contradictory doctrines of "right belief"? The essence of the quandary is this: Many if not most of our spiritual paths have, at least at one time or another, preached that they hold the one and only right answer to the question of God, that theirs is the one and only right spiritual path. It is this specific sense of proprietary rightness that I refer to when I use the term "right belief." It is the idea that there is one and only one right way to approach the sacred, only one right way to perceive the holy, only one right way to believe in God, and thus only one right spiritual path. Foundational to Interfaith is that *there is no one right spiritual path*. How can we reconcile this?

Interfaith looks to the essential core of all of our spiritual paths and recognizes that at the core of *all* of them lie the same teachings—that we should love one another, act with compassion and in community. At its simplest, this is expressed by what has been called the Golden Rule, which can be found woven into every spiritual path, on every continent, throughout human history.[1] Interfaith takes as a basic article of faith that these teachings of love, compassion, and community are what lie at the core of the sacred, not our doctrinal and dogmatic differences. This deceptively simple article of faith is, in fact, a sea change in how we relate both to the sacred and to each other. Our differences are not to be ignored but neither should they be elevated above what ought to unite us.

Interfaith, then, looks to what all of our spiritual paths agree upon, what might be called orthopraxy or "right action." Orthopraxy is all about what we do. Interfaith honors and respects the many differing beliefs and spiritual practices that can lead us to right action but does not believe or accept that there is one particular right belief that will lead to that right action.[2]

Thus Interfaith, as a faith, teaches us that all our spiritual paths are important and have the potential to lead us to our common sacred goal of love, compassion, and community. But what then do we make of the varying doctrines and dogmas that make each of our spiritual paths unique? How is it that Interfaith calls on us to treat these sometimes vastly different doctrines and dogmas with equal respect, without any sense of hierarchy?

A Bit Deeper

Questions for Discussion

Given that sharing our deeply personal spiritual thoughts can make us feel vulnerable, what kind of covenant of respect might we agree to, so that we may share freely without judging or being judged?

In what ways is your spiritual path a religion?

If your chosen spiritual path is a religion, what would make it less of a religion but still a spiritual path? Or if your chosen spiritual path is not a religion, what would make it more of a religion?

Using the analogy of our spiritual paths being sacred language, what are some expressions that are unique to the language of your spiritual path?

Most of our spiritual paths have, at one time or another, held a sense of proprietary rightness—that our path is the one right way to approach the sacred and the one right belief about God. How has your chosen path expressed this "We're right" attitude? Why do you think so many differing paths have felt this one-and-only attitude? How do you think this attitude might be overcome?

2

GUIDES OR
RULEBOOKS?

I live in Lynnwood, Washington, which is north of Seattle. Let's say, as I have a feeling that some of my friends who live in Seattle may actually believe, that the spiritual purpose of life is to get to Seattle. To help people do this, I gather a group around me and we uncover the best route. If the freeway is not jammed, it's best to take I-5 south. Over time, some of us will exit at Mercer, some at Denny, some at James. Moreover, there are alternate routes for snowy days or days with traffic accidents. And while most of us will drive, some will take a bus and a few brave souls will ride bicycles. But *all* our directions for getting to Seattle involve going south. So we write it all down and put it in our sacred book.

But what about the folks who live in Tacoma, who need to travel north, not south, to get to Seattle? If people who dwell in Tacoma pick up our sacred book and think of it as the one undisputed, revealed word about Seattle, they will drive south on I-5. They will reach Oregon, then California, then Mexico, and if they really stick with it, they may eventually end up at the bottom of South America, looking out toward the Antarctic. But they are never going to make it to Seattle by driving south on I-5.

And, of course, for the people who live in Hawaii, Asia, Europe, Africa, or Australia, a sacred book that demands you drive south on I-5 makes no sense whatsoever.

Yet for those of us who live in Lynnwood, our sacred book is indeed helpful. If we follow it, it will help us to make the journey to Seattle. At least it does now that I-5 exists. There was a time when a person needed to take a different path to Seattle, and perhaps the journey was only made possible on horseback. So how helpful would it be to me today to have a sacred book written at that time directing me to Seattle by horseback trails? Yet are these old ways to Seattle now false paths simply because we no longer use them?

What exploring this dilemma is all about is helping us to understand that there are two very different aspects to all our spiritual paths. The first aspect answers the spiritually profound questions: "How am I called to act?" and "What am I called to be as a human being?" Here all our spiritual paths—throughout history, on every continent, in every culture—are in agreement. We are called to be compassionate and loving toward each other, and to live in community. Life is about "us," not just "me" or even "my tribe." From an Interfaith perspective, it is this first aspect that is the crucial one.

The second aspect of our spiritual paths concerns how we might become such a spiritually enlightened human. We need help. There's little doubt about that. We need direction. Little doubt about that, either. This is why we need guidebooks. And it is in our guidebooks that our spiritual paths have diverged wildly. So doctrine—the specific beliefs and practices held and taught by a religion—enters the picture. Interfaith sees doctrine as a guide. Doctrine as a guide can be wonderful, soul-engaging, and spirit-filling, but in the end it is still only a guide. When doctrine becomes law, it can become inflexible and destructive. Much too often this is precisely what has happened within our spiritual paths.

That is, we have allowed doctrine to become more important than the reason for the doctrine: to be loving, compassionate, and in community with our fellow humans and all creatures great and small. To return to our metaphor, we allow arguments over how best to reach Seattle to keep us from actually getting there. We who live north of Seattle hate, disparage, and indeed may go to war with the people who live south of Seattle over whose guidebook to Seattle is right.

How could this happen?

The Need for a Prayer

Let's use the name "Lynnwood" again. But this time let's suppose that a small and isolated village called Lynnwood finds itself divided and hurting and in need of a way to come together in love. The spiritual leaders of Lynnwood create the "Lynnwood Prayer." It's agreed on by all the spiritual leaders, and those who follow them, that a person will get down on one knee and pray for unity and love.

> O healing power of the universe, our souls are troubled. Abide in us. O healing power of the universe, we are divided and fight amongst each other. Help us to find unity and peace. O healing power of the universe, we act hatefully toward one another. Help us to embrace love.

This is to be said three times, with a five-minute interval of silent reflection after each recitation of the prayer. Then the person stands.

The people of Lynnwood realize that they need to do something to attain the peace they lack. They try the prayer and it works. There is peace and unity ... for a time.

From Guide to Doctrine

But now one group in Lynnwood rallies around a new spiritual leader who says that the prayer should be to God and not some "healing power of the universe." The leader declares that not to say "God" is offensive to God. Thus the only correct way to pray the prayer is to say "O God" and not "O healing power of the universe." This becomes how the majority utters the Lynnwood Prayer. Soon those citizens who say "O healing power" become isolated. Not long after that they are distrusted.

Later, another group in Lynnwood rallies around a different spiritual leader. This leader declares that praying on one knee is offensive to God. It blasphemes God. The only true way to say the prayer so that God will accept it is to pray on both knees.

So now there are three separate groups who say the Lynnwood Prayer, but the people of each group insist that their way is the only right way. The groups don't talk much to each other, and when they do speak it is frequently with great disrespect. Clearly the groups no longer pray the Lynnwood Prayer together. How can they? They have three different and mutually exclusive ways of praying that prayer.

The result? Once again, the city of Lynnwood is divided and hurting and in need of a way out.

How on earth did this simple prayer for unity become divisive? It became divisive because *how* to say the prayer had become more important than the *reason* for the prayer. The prayer had ceased to be the guide it was intended to be to help people live in unity and embrace love. Instead, the prayer and the specifics of how to pray it had become an end in and of itself. Prayer has become encrusted with doctrine.

This is how our guidebooks become dogma. But it doesn't explain another important question. If our Scriptures all agree about how we are to act toward each other, *and they do,* why then did our doctrines and dogmas turn out to be so very different?

A Bit Deeper

Questions for Discussion

How would you describe the difference between a sacred guidebook and a sacred rulebook?

In your own spiritual path, what are some examples of how your Scripture (or sacred texts) act as a guidebook? What are some examples of how it acts as a rulebook?

What are some specific ways that your spiritual path calls you to move beyond "me" and reach out to honor others through love, compassion, and community?

What are some examples of your path's doctrine (rules) that make you uncomfortable? Does the doctrine make you uncomfortable or is it the goal of the doctrine that makes you uneasy? Why do you think so?

List some examples of your path's doctrine (rules) that give you comfort. Do you think it is the doctrine itself or the goal of the doctrine that reassures you? Why do you think so?

Have you or someone you know challenged a doctrine in your place of worship? What was the reaction? How did you feel about that?

3

WHY ARE OUR PATHS SO DIFFERENT?

It's worth noting that a perplexing dichotomy permeates humanity's encounters with the sacred. On the one hand, there is the common goal, the worldwide and ageless call to compassion, love, and community. On the other hand, there is the worldwide and ageless absence of agreement about the nature of God (or even agreement about whether God exists), as well as what our proper relationship with God or the sacred should be. It's worth pondering. We have unity about how we are called to treat each other, but disunity about how we are called to pray. What on earth, if you'll excuse the expression, are we supposed to make of that?

In *The Interfaith Alternative,* I suggested that this dichotomy should help us to understand what is truly important.[1] If God, or Conscience, or however we encounter the sacred, has managed to make it crystal clear to all of humanity how we are to act toward each other and yet has left how we are to pray a complete muddle, shouldn't that give us a pretty good clue as to what dwells at the core of the sacred and what doesn't?

Yet even that understanding begs the question of why our spiritual paths relate to the sacred so differently.

The Nature of Our Differences

Once we understand that the doctrines and dogmas that permeate our spiritual paths are not ends in themselves but guides—sacred offerings to help us become more loving and compassionate—it becomes perfectly

11

logical that our spiritual paths would be so different in some ways and so similar in others. Consider how differently the call to a path of love, compassion, and community would need to be framed; the sorts of examples used; and the philosophies that support it, if they're expressed from the point of view of a long-established Asian culture as opposed to the point of view of a tribe wandering the sands of Sinai.

But isn't Scripture the Word of God? Some may argue that it isn't, but let us assume that Scripture is indeed the Word of God. What we much too often forget is that it is the Word of God as understood by the ears of humanity. Does that make a difference? I believe it makes a significant difference.

As human beings, we are only capable of understanding what our knowledge and experience *allow* us to understand. Thus the Word of God can only be understood according to ears of the time and place that hear it.

Let's take as an example something from my own spiritual tradition. Imagine that Moses, the lawgiver and great prophet of Judaism, has just received the Decalogue, the Ten Commandments. Moses and God sit down afterward for a friendly chat, as God answers a few of Moses's most pressing questions.

"How did you create us?" Moses asks. This is a hugely important question. Where did we come from is something that every human being and indeed every culture wants to know. God obligingly replies.

"First, Moses, you need to understand that you are made up of billions upon billions of atoms."

"What?!"

"I know you think your body is solid, but actually you are mostly space. And these billions of atoms that form the you that is Moses are constantly in motion—even now, as you sit absolutely still, your atoms are all moving."

"What?!" Moses exclaims. "Lord, with all due respect, that makes no sense at all!"

"Hmm. OK. Let me simplify. Billions of years ago ..."

"What? Billions? What's that?" Recall that Moses lived at a time when the children of Israel were illiterate. I think there is divine logic in a Decalogue, ten commandments that can be counted on the fingers of both hands.

God realizes that things have to be made even simpler.

"OK. Understand, Moses, that a very, very long time ago, there was no universe. None of this existed. I created a Big Bang and ..."

"A big what?"

"OK. OK. See all those little twinkly lights up there in the sky? They aren't just twinkly lights, Moses. I know you think that the earth is the center of everything, but it's not. Those are planets, stars, and galaxies up there. Much of the light you are seeing is billions of years ... uh, is very, very old. And Moses, you know the light is old because the speed of light is constant and most of those stars and galaxies are very, very far away."

"What's a planet? What's a star? What's a galaxy? The speed of light? Light has a speed? Like when I run, rather than walk? Lord, I don't understand. I don't understand any of this. Please, please just tell me ... how did you create us?"

"OK. OK. Let's try this, Moses. In the beginning, I created the heaven and the earth."

"Got it."

I realize that this begins to read like a Bill Cosby monologue. It is not my purpose to make light of anyone's spiritual path—which is why I drew this example from my own. My point is that there is no way for God to explain quantum mechanics to Moses. In plain truth, it's hard enough for us to grasp it today. So we see that however inerrant and perfect God's Word may be, that word has to be interpreted by the ears that hear it, and thus Scripture, even if it begins as the inerrant Word of God, must be a creature of the time in which it was written. It has to conform to the knowledge, the science, the experience, and the cultural norms of the people receiving it, or it will make no sense.

We who read Scripture today possess a different knowledge and science, different experiences, and differing cultural norms from those who lived two thousand years before us. Even the most fundamentalist of our spiritual paths today, the most orthodox of Orthodox Jews, the most conservative of Christians, Muslims, Hindus, and whomever, try as they might, cannot escape the fact that they live in the twenty-first century. It's a big universe out there, and there is no way to make it small again. The universe that Moses and the Hebrews of his time understood has disappeared forever.

Indeed, one of the most difficult and traumatic spiritual experiences is trying to reconcile the limits of science and knowledge of yesterday, that are of necessity embedded in Scripture, with the science and knowledge of today. But should it be that difficult and traumatic?

It is time to remember, and perhaps reflect a bit, that the very reason for Scripture is to help and guide us so that we may practice the great commandment of God to love each other, to act with compassion and in community. But how God tries to help us get there, and the nature of how our guidebooks are framed, will depend on our worldview. How could it not? The Scripture we receive will depend on the ears we have to hear it. And those ears will be different at different times, on different continents, and in different cultures.

The Effect of Our Worldview

In Hebrew Scripture Cain asks, "Am I my brother's keeper?" (Genesis 4:9). But why? Aren't our sisters equally important? I think so. Yet most of Hebrew Scripture is based on the cultural norm of patriarchy, which was at that time the Hebrew worldview. But that does not mean that we have to or indeed should embrace that ancient worldview today.

I deeply believe that the point of Hebrew Scripture is not that men are naturally the heads of households and women should be obedient wives and homemakers. I believe that the point of Hebrew Scripture is that we should love one another, act with compassion and in community. As the Talmud phrases it, "The whole of the Torah is for the purpose of promoting peace" (*Gittin* 59b). That this was framed in terms of a patriarchy in Hebrew Scripture reflects the time when the Scripture was written down, not God's will.

Yet to this day, patriarchy rears its ugly head. Genesis, as example, has two creation stories. In one, God creates man and woman on the sixth day, both in God's image, and God blesses them both equally (Genesis 1:26–28). In the other story, God only creates man (Adam) from the dust of the earth, and it is only when God feels that man should not be alone, and that all the creatures of the earth just aren't enough company for Adam, that God finally creates Eve, not from the dust of the earth but from Adam's rib (Genesis 2:18–22). Yet which story is the one so many people remember? It is the story that has Eve created from Adam and, not coincidentally, Eve immediately succumbs to the wiles of the serpent and gets Adam kicked out of Eden. But does this reflect God's view of Eve or the patriarchal view of the Hebrews? That becomes a pivotal question.

I believe that the answer to that question depends on the answer we give to a mostly unasked but truly foundational question. Would God, with this clarion and eternal call to love, compassion, and community, only speak of this call to a tribe wandering around in the Sinai desert and leave out everyone else on the planet? Would God truly ignore all the people in Asia, India, Africa, Europe, and everywhere else on earth in order to whisper only to the children of Israel, and then sit back and wait, knowing that the word would slowly leak out over the next millennium or two?

Let me be as clear as I possibly can. This is most assuredly *not* to say that God did not speak to Moses. I personally believe that God did indeed speak to Moses. But this *is* to say, and it is a fundamental tenet of Interfaith, that God did not speak *only* to Moses.

I'm reminded of Christian Scripture, where an increasingly frustrated Jesus tries to guide his disciples with parable after parable. But time after time, the disciples get bogged down in the details of the parable and miss the point. God, or Conscience, or Spirit, or however we may encounter the sacred has given us what amounts to parable after parable after parable: our varying Scriptures. Like the disciples, we get bogged down in the details of the parable and miss the point: Love each other—for crying out loud, *love* each other!

So, why are our spiritual paths so different? They are different because we are different. This is why one of the great underpinnings of Interfaith is the call for each of us to find a spiritual path that will help us be a better human being. For some that path will be of the Baha'i, for others the path of Sikhism, for others the path of "I don't know yet–ism," or one of the other multitude of paths, all of which present us with the opportunity to be better human beings. The question for Interfaith, then, is not which path is right, but which path will help each of us as a special, important, and unique human being best realize our humanity?

A Bit Deeper

Questions for Discussion

Say you were traveling in the desert where water is scarce. How might you describe compassion to a person who lives there? How might your description change if you were describing compassion to a person who lived in a land filled with rivers and lakes?

Have you ever misheard the lyrics to a song or a poem and only later learned that the words were not what you thought? Could you share some examples? What would have happened if you'd written the words down when you first heard them and then passed those words on to the next generation?

What might be some evidence from your spiritual tradition that shows it originated in a time much different from our own?

What are some ways in which your spiritual community clashes with the twenty-first century, or perhaps you in your practices or beliefs find yourself in conflict with the modern world?

4

WHAT WE CALL IT MATTERS

In effective communication, the language we choose is crucial. So before we continue, there's a reasonable question to answer. It's a question I've been asked more than once. Why use the word "Interfaith" with a capital "I"? Is this an accident? Carelessness? Laziness? Whimsy? There are a multitude of other words not only available but currently in use. Four of the most common are "multifaith," "multireligious," "interreligious," and "interfaith" (set lowercase). Why not use any or all of these? After all, as Shakespeare has Juliet tell Romeo, "What's in a name? That which we call a rose by any other name would smell as sweet."

First, words actually do mean something. As example, while a rose by any other name might indeed smell as sweet, if someone is handing you a flower, knowing it's a rose can help you avoid being stabbed by thorns in the stem. Moreover, regardless of fragrance, if we call a rose a tulip we're going to confuse the heck out of anyone with eyes to see, not to mention the person who may know what a tulip actually smells like.

So, why Interfaith?

Let's do this in steps. Given our very human habit of using comparisons as value judgments, let's begin first with the understanding that there is nothing at all wrong with the words "multireligious" and "multifaith." The question at hand is not, Are these good or bad words? Rather, What word will most accurately describe what it is we are trying to talk about?

Why Faith?

OK then, why choose the word "faith" rather than "religious"? This is per-haps the easiest delineation because we've already dealt with it earlier in this book. "Religious" speaks to me of religion, and thus of doctrines, dog-mas, and precise, organized ways of dealing with the sacred. Each reli-gion has its own language. Indeed, as already mentioned, I see religions as languages for speaking to and about the sacred.[1] "Faith" speaks to me of a much more general, deeply held conviction about the sacred. Thus our faith might move us to pray, but it won't establish how we should pray. Religion will establish doctrines about prayer, such as when we pray and whether we should be on one knee or both knees. Should our heads be covered and, if so, how? Should men and women be separate when they pray? Again, it is not that "religion" is wrong or bad. Rather, for me, "faith" better captures what we have been and will be talking about. As example, Interfaith teaches that if you feel called to cover your head when you pray, you are to be respected in doing so. If you do not feel called to cover your head when you pray, you are to be respected in not doing so.

Why Interfaith (with a capital "I")?

But if we've decided on "faith," then why not "multifaith" or "interfaith"? Why Interfaith, with a capital "I"?

Let's first look at the prefix "multi." For me, "multifaith" conjures up different faiths coming together simply and solely as different faiths. The phrase "separate but equal" comes to mind. What I want to be talking about here is "different, but related" rather than "separate but equal" and that's "inter," not "multi."

If this all seems just a bit esoteric, perhaps an example will help. What comes to mind when you think of something as multiconnected? For me, that conjures up a giant hub with any number of different things plugged into it. They may be related or they may not. Imagine you have an exten-sion cord with room for plugs from three different electrical devices. One device might be a clock, another your television, and the last a lamp. The lamp, the clock, and the television are all connected to the same extension cord. They are multiconnected, but they are not interconnected.

So what comes to mind when you think of something as interconnected? For me, it's any number of seemingly separate things that are all part of a greater whole. They may be similar or quite different, but they are still part of the whole. Let's go back to our example of an extension cord. Let's say that an amplifier, some speakers, and a CD player are connected. If you only have the amplifier, you'll hear nothing. If you only have a speaker, you'll hear nothing. If you put a CD into the player, but don't have an amplifier and speaker, you'll hear nothing. But if you put them all together, you can at last hear the CDs. The amplifier, CD player, and speakers are interconnected.

If we espouse *inter*faith, it means that we see our spiritual paths as interconnected, interrelated. This does not mean we are interchangeable! To say our spiritual paths are all related does not mean they are all the same. Are you the same as your brother or sister? Are you the same as your aunts, uncles, or cousins? Of course not. Nonetheless, you are related; you are part of the same family. Interfaith acknowledges the many differing paths that the human family, as a family, walks as it seeks the sacred.

Lastly, why "Interfaith," with a capital "I," rather than "interfaith"? This requires a bit of history. I really enjoy the *Oxford English Dictionary* (OED) because it not only defines words but also tries to find when the word entered the English language, at least in print. You won't find the word "interfaith" in the OED until the 1970s. When you do, the entry references a late 1960s journal that speaks of an interfaith march, in this case for workers' rights issues in the United Kingdom.

There's no way to prove it, but I have long held the conviction that the word "interfaith" owes much to the work of the Reverend Dr. Martin Luther King Jr., who brought together people from all faiths to march for civil rights. That these were interfaith activities was both clear and clearly new. Somewhere along the line, the word "interfaith" was coined to describe this coming together of differing faiths in common purpose.

Yet I think it's also important to recognize what these marches were not. People marched and went home. A few people of differing faiths may or may not have discussed their spiritual paths. But if there was any discussion, there wasn't much. This does not in any way diminish the importance of these interfaith marches for civil rights and social justice. They were what they were intended to be—interfaith marches for civil rights and social justice.

But the idea of interfaith dialogue soon followed. Interfaith dialogue has its own history. Though it wasn't termed "interfaith" yet, such dialogue might be traced back to the first Parliament of the World's Religions in

1893. Not every world religion, let alone spiritual path, was included. But it was a start, a beginning of interfaith conversation.

Until then, any dialogue between the faiths was pretty much limited to conversations along the line of, "I'm right, and you're going to hell. Let's talk!" The Parliament of the World's Religions didn't end that sort of thing,[2] but it did begin a movement away from it. The Second Vatican Council (1962–1965) allowed Catholicism to take a new look at, among many other things, its relationship with the other religious paths of the world. Particularly in 1965, the church moved toward real dialogue with other religions (though not so much other faiths), and particularly with Judaism. This was due in part to the *Nostra Aetate* declaration, an outgrowth of the Second Vatican Council that revolutionized the Catholic church's approach to Jews and Judaism after nearly two thousand years of antagonism and, much too frequently, violence.[3]

Up to the publication of *The Interfaith Alternative* in 2012, the word "interfaith" was used almost entirely in these two very important ways—relating to either interfaith action, meaning a number of differing faiths coming together to accomplish a task, or interfaith dialogue, meaning at least two differing spiritual paths talking to each other, with the accent more on understanding each other than converting a perceived wrong-believer.

So "interfaith" was an adjective. It described a kind of action or dialogue. This use of the word should be respected and honored. Much of great value has been accomplished through both interfaith action and interfaith dialogue.

For me, then, the question became how to delineate interfaith as a faith. I chose to follow the example of Christianity, Judaism, Islam, Buddhism, Humanism, and so many others. Thus, Interfaith.

A Bit Deeper

Questions for Discussion

What cautions might we take in comparing definitions of words that describe our spiritual feelings without making judgments? How might we, as example, define and compare "faith" and "religion" so that we may discuss them without ending up with one as "better" than the other?

One possible help might be to compare using bricks to build a house as opposed to wood. Are you able to talk about the strengths and weaknesses of each approach without declaring that one is "better" than the other?

How would you explain the difference between "Interfaith" and "interfaith"?

How would you explain the difference between "multireligious" and "multifaith"?

5

A Blasphemous Look at Blasphemy

The concept of blasphemy has been with us since, well, the beginning. No sooner did humanity come to some idea about God than it seems that the idea of blasphemy reared its ugly head. *Webster's* tells us that blasphemy is "the act of insulting or showing contempt or lack of reverence for God." Blasphemy can be punishable by ostracism, torture, or even death. Even today, though I hesitate to use the word "even," little seems to be able to rile the faithful more fervently than what is perceived as blasphemy.

But have you ever wondered, "Is God really that thin-skinned?" I have.

I believe in a loving and accepting God. I can't believe that God suffers from such low self-esteem that all hell will break loose, literally, if we don't show the proper respect in the proper way—not to mention that what is considered the proper respect in the proper way varies from era to era, culture to culture, and spiritual path to spiritual path. As previously observed, some of us find it essential to cover our head when we pray. For others, that is wholly unnecessary. Are the people who cover their head out of respect for God silly? I don't think so. Are the people who don't cover their head being disrespectful to God? I don't think so. So what's going on?

An Affront to God?

The truth of it is that the concept of blasphemy has little or nothing to do with God or the spiritual. But it has everything to do with politics, the preservation of power, and the attempt to gain power.

I recall as a child engaging in a moderately heated discussion with my father. Dad believed in the righteous power of the fist. I never have. When I was about ten I asked my dad—and yes, I know I'm dating myself—"If I say Sandy Koufax is the greatest pitcher in baseball and you say he isn't, and you beat me up, does that make me wrong? And if somehow I beat you up, does that make me right?" Dad was a tad flummoxed and had no answer.

I was elated some months later when our family happened to watch *The Big Country* on television. If you haven't seen the movie, Gregory Peck and Charlton Heston are antagonists until near the end. Finally, they have an epic fistfight, which leaves the two men on their knees having beaten each other to a draw. Peck's character asks, "Tell me. What did we prove?" The answer is clear. They've proven nothing.

If God exists, and I scream that God does not exist, will that make God disappear? I don't think so. And if God does not exist, and I scream that God does exist, will this somehow create God? Again, I don't think so. And if I pull out a knife, gun, or bomb, it changes nothing. Violence will neither create God nor make God disappear, even if we're willing to annihilate thousands upon thousands attempting to prove our point.

So what does one person's willingness to hate or torture or kill another over blasphemy tell us about the strength of the avenger's belief in God? If you assert that it means the person is a strong believer, I would counter that it shows very much the opposite.

If one human tortures or kills another because that person believes the other has angered God, I would suggest that that human's faith in God is weak, not strong. God does not need us to hate, torture, or kill for God's sake. If we think about it a moment or two, doesn't it seem strange that we would believe in a God of love who nonetheless demands that we be relentlessly unforgiving, and that we hate or even kill each other?

I would submit that blasphemy as an affront to God does not exist. Whoever and whatever God may be or seem to be, surely God, and most particularly a loving God, doesn't need humans to protect the faith, let alone protect it with hatred and violence.

The Truth about Blasphemy

So if blasphemy is not an affront to God, what is it? That, for me, is the more interesting and enlightening question. I believe blasphemy is an affront to power—human power, not God's—and to the humans who seek not only to make the rules but also to ensure that they alone control who makes the rules. It is this desire to protect and project power over others that provokes such anger and violence. If we have learned nothing else from history, we ought to have learned by now that those in power want to stay in power. Those who seek power, but feel they have none, rely on accusations of blasphemy as well to provide an emotional cudgel to help them gain control and authority. A lamentable truth is that humanity learned long ago that little in this life better protects a person's power, or helps a person to grab power from someone else, than control over a community's spiritual life.

Thus, when spiritual leaders tell you something is blasphemous, what they are really saying is that they feel threatened by it. When spiritual leaders call upon their followers to rise up in violent protest over blasphemy, I believe that it has everything to do with power and nothing whatsoever to do with God.

Whenever we feel even the first twinge of self-righteous spiritual thought, let alone feel called to action against another in the name of God, let us learn to ask, "What would a God of love ask of me?" I sincerely doubt the answer to that will be to hate or murder.

What then do we do about our differences? Interfaith teaches us that we need to respect them—not tolerate, but respect. If my brother is called to face Mecca when he prays, what I am called to do is respect his beliefs. If my sister is called to cross herself, what I am called to do is respect her beliefs. If my brother is called to a life of compassion and community with no thought of God, what I am called to do is respect his beliefs. I don't happen to face Mecca or cross myself when I pray, and I do believe in God. But what Interfaith has taught me is to respect the spiritual paths of my brothers and sisters, not to judge them.

Yet the cold truth is that it can be hard to respect a faith when you know little or nothing about it. This is where an Interfaith church can be both helpful and fulfilling. In an Interfaith church, we celebrate each other's spiritual paths and holy days—not to convert or convince, but, rather, to share and to honor each other in the sharing.

More than that, Interfaith, as a faith, has some profound implications not only for our spiritual selves but also for our daily life. It is time to consider day-to-day Interfaith.

A Bit Deeper

Questions for Discussion

Since a cornerstone of Interfaith is respect, how would you differentiate between blasphemy and not showing respect for another person's beliefs?

Why do you think accusations of blasphemy have been so effective in silencing dissent throughout history?

Have you ever thought something was blasphemous? If so, what was it? Why did you feel it was blasphemous?

Voices of Interfaith

Cathy Merchant

Everyone in my immediate family was Roman Catholic, so I was raised with a solid foundation in the church. As a family, we would say the rosary together after dinner every evening, go to confession every Saturday, and attend mass together on Sundays. I loved this routine as a child and felt very nourished and content in my spiritual life. Over the years, I became more involved in our local church and eventually grew quite close to our priest, who was an exceptionally personable and compassionate man. I enjoyed many thought-provoking religious conversations with him throughout my teens; these continued until I went away to college.

Honestly, if I had stayed in my hometown, I probably would have remained Catholic indefinitely, but the Catholic community in my college town was much less welcoming and I felt ostracized for my political and social views. After a year and a half of spiritual dissatisfaction, I left the faith and began studying other religions in earnest. I organized a Buddhist study group with one of my professors and started practicing Tibetan Buddhist meditation and prayer on a regular basis. I also began attending synagogue with my then–boyfriend, who was Jewish, and fell in love with the Hebrew prayers and rituals that have somehow lasted for thousands of years. We studied Jewish texts together and went to temple every Friday for years, after which point we moved to a new area and I began the extensive conversion process to Judaism. However, the synagogues in our new community were considerably more traditional and my rabbi's vehement distrust of non-Jews ultimately led me to end my conversion. After much soul searching, I eventually felt drawn to the compassion and peacefulness expressed in Mahayana Buddhism. I officially joined a *sangha* and "converted." I haven't looked back since.

I met Steven Greenebaum at an interfaith conference, just a few weeks before the first official Living Interfaith service. When he told me about his plan to create an Interfaith church that was open to members of all religious backgrounds, I was intrigued. It reminded me of some Baha'i interfaith gatherings I had attended in the past, and I loved the idea of being able to resume the study of other faiths while still remaining firmly set in my own. I was also happy to hear that my own family would be welcome, as there are not very many places where I may worship with both my father (who is still Christian) and my husband (who is Muslim). The three of us began attending immediately and have since happily celebrated Christmas, Buddha Day, and Ramadan together. Living Interfaith really is an amazing community, and I am very grateful to have found it.

Gloria Parker

My parents were not members of any established church, so I was not raised within a particular belief system or the structure of a given church. Many of my extended family belonged to specific churches, such as Lutheran and Catholic, and I was familiar with these churches during my youth and adulthood. My parents celebrated the various Christian holidays, Easter and Christmas, but not within a religious context. Our moral instruction was mostly common courtesy, good manners, and the Golden Rule.

As I got older I wanted to know more about the beliefs of others as I explored my own religious and spiritual nature. I began reading and talking with others. I was married in the Catholic church since my husband was raised in the church and wanted to honor his parents by marrying there, though he wasn't an active Catholic. As a young parent, I was active in a Lutheran church for a few years and had my children in Sunday School and Vacation Bible School. It wasn't where I wanted to be and moved on. When my husband was terminally ill, we became active in some friends' Baptist church. I liked the people and they were good to my husband during his illness, but the minister wasn't really interested in helping me through my grief and chose to ignore my need for spiritual support. I left that church and a few years later became a member of a Unitarian Universalist church. It was closer to what I needed in my spiritual journey, but not quite.

I joined Living Interfaith Church because I believe that all of our paths have profound things to teach us as well as contradictions, and I don't want to be limited by a single path. I have found my spiritual home in a mixture of faiths and teachings found within Interfaith. I enjoy and feel nurtured by the wide diversity of faiths within the membership of Living Interfaith Church. It's my spiritual home.

Part II

DAY-TO-DAY
INTERFAITH

6

THE DECISION TO ACT

Most if not all of us have at one point or another come across some version of that old bromide, "Wishing will not make it so." In large part, the reason for writing this book is that wishing for Interfaith will not make it so. We have to decide to make it so, and then *act* to make it so.

Interfaith, like every other faith, needs intent. Protestations of loyalty, and proclamations about its inclusivity and power to heal, however eloquent, aren't particularly relevant.[1] The hard truth is that we can neither proclaim nor deny the sacred by a statement of our beliefs. We proclaim or deny the sacred by our actions. A commitment is made. Then it is followed up ... or not.

Still, however much we may feel called to something, whenever we are asked for a commitment a very reasonable question arises. We will likely want to inquire, "Just what is it that I'm being asked to commit to?" So let's explore what we are committing to if we decide to commit to Interfaith as a faith. What is being asked of us? Just as important, what isn't being asked of us?

First, when you commit to Interfaith as a faith you become an Interfaither rather than an Interfaithist. This is more than semantics. It is basic. "Interfaithist" conjures up adherence to a long list of doctrines and dogmas. An Interfaither is a person who adheres to the core understandings of Interfaith as a faith without regard to specific doctrines or dogmas. As example, an Interfaither might say, "I believe that we are all brothers and sisters called to love, compassion, and community." An Interfaithist might say, "I believe that we are all brothers and sisters, called to love, compassion, and community; and here's the one and only right way to do it!"

Yet there is a profound and, for many, unsettling question that faces the person who finds Interfaith attractive and feels called to it: "What must I give up to become an Interfaither?" This is by far the question I have been asked the most often. No other question even comes close. It's understandable. The paradigm under which we have lived for several thousand years has demanded of us, and still demands, that if we have walked with one spiritual community and decide to walk with another, we must give up the beliefs held by our first community in order to embrace the beliefs of the new one. To join a new spiritual community, we are taught we must resign from the old one.

There is no such paradigm in Interfaith. As an Interfaither, the only belief about the sacred you must let go of is the belief that you're right and anyone who disagrees with you is wrong. "I'm right, and you're going to hell" has no place in Interfaith. Those who cannot let go of the belief that there is only one right answer to the sacred, be they Jewish, Christian, Muslim, Baha'i, Hindu, Buddhist, Humanist, Pagan, or other, will not find a happy or fulfilling home in Interfaith. Those who can let go will find in Interfaith a welcome and nurturing home.

Some of us—indeed most of us—in the beginning will find this much harder to put into practice than to preach. The paradigm of "right belief" has been engraved if not into our DNA then surely into our traditions and some of our earliest teachings as children. Some, at least in the beginning, will find that they can only go as far as to say that they commit to respecting and then practicing respect for our diverse spiritual paths. But they will find that, despite their best efforts, they still hold on to the belief that their own spiritual practice is the most right of all practices—the first, if you will, among equals. That's not a good place to end our journey, but it is a perfectly acceptable place to begin it.

The truth of it is, the more completely we can put the idea of right belief behind us, the happier and more fulfilled we will be in our practice of Interfaith. But knowing that, if it takes us time to get there, we must be ready and willing to take that time. As long as we are willing to recognize the vestiges of right belief within our own minds and hearts, and embrace the need to work on banishing it, Interfaith can and will be a fulfilling spiritual path.

That's it. What Interfaith requires of us is that we place firmly in the dustbin the paradigm that states that there is and can only be one right belief about the sacred. It requires us to broaden our horizons, not narrow them. Interfaith not only moves us past fearing another because that person's spiritual beliefs are different but it also moves us beyond tolerating another person's differing spiritual beliefs. Interfaith teaches us that we need to respect each other's spiritual paths, not merely tolerate them.

A commitment to Interfaith, then, is a commitment to respecting other beliefs, even if we view the sacred differently—even if we view it very differently.

Interfaith further teaches us that while beliefs are important, we must pay much closer attention to the actions those beliefs prompt. As example, Islam is to be respected. Al-Qaeda terrorists are not. Christianity is to be respected. Christian Identity terrorists are not. Judaism is to be respected. Kach terrorists are not. Lamentably, one could go on and on.

This all comes back to something we've observed before. For each of us, as individuals, what we believe is crucial, for what we believe becomes the foundation for who we are. But always, always, as a community, it is what we do with our beliefs that counts.

Thus a part of the commitment to Interfaith is a commitment to put the fear of "other" aside. To commit to Interfaith is to commit to the belief that we are all brothers and sisters, with diverse approaches to the sacred, and then to practice that belief, even when we disagree—especially when we disagree.[2]

So a commitment to Interfaith is no small commitment. Nor is it an easy commitment. But I do believe it can be a rewarding and healing one. Interfaith widens our world. And, if we will let it, Interfaith frees us from the imprisoning shackles of one of the most debilitating of all human emotions—fear of the "other."

What then do we gain as we embrace Interfaith? The need to convert or convince others of the rightness of our beliefs disappears. The need to defend our beliefs against contrary beliefs disappears as well. Perhaps more important even than these, we begin to understand our brothers and sisters at a level not previously open to us. It will not follow automatically, and it will not follow without work, but we can begin to prepare the way for us to practice the love, compassion, and community that all of our spiritual paths have told us are our most sacred goals.

Commitment to Interfaith is a difficult commitment, but it is a commitment worth making. Just how difficult? Let's take a deeper look at that.

A Bit Deeper

Questions for Discussion

What are some of the "We're right" beliefs of your own spiritual path? How might you let go of "We're right" without letting go of the aspects of your spiritual path that call to you?

What other examples of a possible difference between an Interfaither and an Interfaithist can you come up with?

What examples from your own life reveal the difference between showing "tolerance" and showing "respect"?

How do you hear people differently when you respect them, rather than merely tolerating them?

WHY INTERFAITH CAN BE HARD

Writer, poet, and sometime theologian G. K. Chesterton famously wrote, "The Christian ideal has not been tried and found wanting. It has been found difficult; and left untried."[1] I think the same may well be said of each and every one of our spiritual paths. Loving one another, acting with compassion toward one another, and acting in community is very easy to proclaim yet, as humanity has discovered over and over again, it is very difficult to live. Now comes Interfaith onto the scene, telling us that not only should Christian embrace Christian, but also Buddhist. Not only should Jew embrace Jew, but also Muslim. Not only should Baha'i embrace Baha'i, but also Humanist. Interfaith calls on us not only to understand, but also to embrace that we are all one family, with no branch of that family having the single right answer to the sacred.

Is that really so different from where we are today? Unfortunately, but emphatically, yes.

We live today in an us-and-them world—every corner of the globe and in every conceivable way it's "us and them." Nor is this anything new. Indeed, framing the world in terms of "us and them" is very much a holdover from our tribal ancestry, and we remain expert tribalists. The sad truth is that we take any and every possible excuse to divide and then subdivide ourselves. We divide over race, gender, generations, and national boundaries as well as, of course, our spiritual paths—to name only a few of our seemingly endless divisions. But it doesn't stop there. Every spiritual path on earth has divided, then subdivided, and then divided yet again.

Many of our most intractable ills may be laid at the altar of our divisions into "them and us." Such a mind-set—and emotional fixation—allows us to judge others and find them lesser beings. But there is no "them," and there is no "us" who are somehow superior to "them." Nor is there a wrong that is somehow less wrong because it is practiced by "us" against "them."

Rejecting this harmful and hurtful dichotomy, Interfaith teaches that our tribe is humanity. This sounds simple enough. It may even sound attractive. After all, as we well know, some form of the Golden Rule is the cornerstone of every spiritual path that can be found on every continent throughout history. "Do unto others as you would have them do unto you" calls on us not to treat "them" any differently than we would want "us" treated. But the truth is that if embracing our common humanity is doable at all, it will take unwavering intention and work ... hard work.

So, is the practice of Interfaith even possible? Given humanity's track record, this is a reasonable question to ask. I must confess that I'm agnostic. I don't know if it's possible. But I believe it is possible, and believing it I feel compelled to try. More than that, given the morass in which humanity finds itself, I genuinely believe that Interfaith can help to guide us toward the love, compassion, and community that we seek.

It is important then to understand and embrace that Interfaith is not a solution. Interfaith as a faith will not provide an instant end to our problems. Interfaith is not "The Answer." What Interfaith can do is help move us past some huge, centuries-old and hate-encrusted barriers to our goal of compassion and love. Interfaith, if we will embrace and then practice it, shatters the great, unyielding wall of right belief that has divided humanity into "us and them" and left us forever so much smaller than we could be. But again, we need to face a truth. If that wall weren't attractive and useful, at least to most, it wouldn't remain.

"Judge not," Matthew 7:1 cautions us. But we judge all the time. Within the realm of the sacred we are taught to judge the beliefs of others based on our own beliefs. We are taught to judge how others experience the sacred based on our own experiences. To see how unfortunate this is, indulge me in a short parable.

So Who Is Right?

Imagine that one morning you get up and, as you swing out of bed, you realize that you're just a little groggy. "Hmm," you think. "Probably should have skipped that late-night comedy show—but then again, it *was* funny!" You stumble toward the shower, dreaming of that first, wonderful cup of coffee, and you run headfirst into the bathroom door. Bam! It's nothing serious. No blood. But there's a lovely new red crease, right between your eyes—a reminder that sleep really is important.

You make it to work and, sure enough, someone you work with notices that crease on your forehead.

"Aha!" this person says. "I know what happened to you this morning. A little sleep-deprived, were we?"

You nod sheepishly.

"I knew it!" your coworker says. "Don't be embarrassed. The same thing happened to me two weeks ago. Let me tell you what happened. You felt tired. Right? Couldn't really focus your eyes."

"Yeah," you whisper.

"You reached up high for a book on the top shelf of your bookcase, but it slipped and slammed into your forehead. Am I right, or am I right?"

"Well, no," you say, with an embarrassed laugh. "Actually, I ran into the bathroom door."

"No, you didn't!" your coworker tells you. "I know what happened. I had the same experience, so I know what happened. You dropped a book on your head! Why do you deny it?"

"I really did run into the door," you say. "I was there. Trust me, I wouldn't make this up! I ran into the door."

"No! You may *think* you ran into a door, you may even *believe* that you ran into a door, but I know the truth. I know it because it happened to me. You dropped a book on your head! And once you realize the truth, you'll see that I'm right!"

Does this make any sense at all?

I hope not. Your coworker stands in front of you and passionately insists that what you experienced, what you know happened because you were there, in fact *didn't* happen.

If that sounds a little arrogant, consider that this is precisely how we've been discussing our spiritual differences for centuries. A person has an experience of the sacred. Because she or he experienced it, that person knows it's true. And since it's true, anyone who doesn't experience the sacred in the same way must be wrong. It's no laughing matter. One of us encounters the sacred through Buddhism, another through Christianity, another through Islam, or Judaism, or a walk in the forest. And then the argument begins. Who is right?[2]

Our arguments over whose path is right have led to segregation, discrimination, hatred, violence, even war. And it's still happening today. It's happening right now.

Even when our mind tells us not to judge, we have become so conditioned to judging others that even when we believe we are being accepting of another point of view we tend to do so with, at best, a patronizing attitude. "Well, if that's what you need to believe, then you go right ahead." Gee, thanks for the permission!

We have been socialized, conditioned if you will, for intolerance. But why? It goes beyond the broad sweep of tribalism and, in fact, reinforces our perceived need for tribes. There is no easy answer. Indeed, there are many answers. But let's examine a few of the answers that directly affect our spiritual selves. While there may be similarities to other aspects of passing judgment, let's focus on judgment and spirit.

Passing Judgment

We have found countless ways of passing judgment on each other. But I'd like to look at two that seem to me particularly relevant to our discussion.

A Need to Feel Superior

As a teenager, I was rather startled to be introduced to a rationale for judging others that had frankly never occurred to me. I spent a weekend with other teens participating in what was called a spiritual encounter group. It was a fascinating experience for many reasons. But the one that smacked me in the face and has vividly stayed with me over all these years came at one of our last sessions. A member of our group admitted to being prejudiced. He wasn't happy about it, but he wasn't ready to put it behind him, either. I can no longer remember what group he was feeling superior to, but I do remember asking him, "Since you know it's wrong, can't you let go of it?"

He looked straight at me and said with passion and no little anguish, "No! I have to feel that I'm better than *somebody*. I have to!"

You could have knocked me over with that proverbial feather. He felt so small, so insignificant. I doubt I was familiar with the term "self-worth" in those days, but clearly, for a reason I couldn't fathom, he felt all but worthless. Singling out a class of people, a "them" who were by definition less than he, allowed him a feeling of self-worth that he otherwise could not find. As I got older and had more opportunities to study history and the world around me, I realized he was not alone. One important factor in our willingness to judge others is our own insecurity, our deep and relentless doubts about our own value as human beings. Judging others gives us power and a feeling of worth. It's nothing to be laughed at or sneered at. It's real, it's more prevalent than we may realize, and we need to understand it.[3] It plays an important role in the attitude underlying this statement: "I may be a failure, but God loves me. God loves *me* and not you!" If I believe that, it gives me importance. It gives me worth. And, tragically, it gives me the right to treat you like dirt.

For thousands of years we've allowed a poisonous paradigm to provide a foundation for our spiritual beliefs. That paradigm says that there is one and only one right spiritual path—only one right belief about God and the sacred. Yet, as we move to put right belief behind us, we need to understand that in many ways right belief has frequently functioned as a spiritual life jacket for the oppressed. No matter what else may happen, no matter how horrific our lives, we can take heart because God will reward "us" and damn "them." It should be clear then that embracing Interfaith is not possible unless at the same moment we truly embrace justice for our entire human family.

If You're Right, I'm Wrong

There's an even darker side to right belief. Consider the shattering risk that any real discussion of our spiritual paths can bring with it. If we talk, and if there is only one right belief, and if your belief begins to make sense to me, then my beliefs must be wrong. And if my beliefs are wrong, my life and perhaps my parents' lives have been without meaning. With this much at stake, if I face someone who believes differently than I do, and if I embrace the idea that there can only be one right belief, I have a very real reason for holding my hands against my ears and not listening.

Moreover, if my spiritual identity depends on your being wrong, how can we possibly have a genuine exchange of ideas or beliefs? I can't really listen to you. When you speak, the whole of me will be engaged in searching for a point of departure, something I can use against you. I must not only judge you and your spiritual path, but my very survival, my sense of self-worth, demands that I judge you to be in error.

Though largely unspoken, this is one of the most profound barriers to Interfaith. And since it is unspoken, the first step toward moving ahead is to recognize and name it.

The Hard Work of Interfaith

Interfaith then may be easy to preach but much harder to practice. In the next chapter we'll take a look at some practical ways to practice Interfaith. There is no question that Interfaith takes practice—lots of it! So perhaps the most important thing to keep in mind is that it will take time. There will be frustrations along the way and we must not let ourselves be discouraged by them. We'll need to take a breath, gird our loins, and keep going. Respect for and celebration of our differing spiritual paths is not going to happen overnight. But if we keep at it, it will happen.

A Bit Deeper

Questions for Discussion

What might some "us" and "them" examples from your own life be that you may not have thought about before?

How do you tend to judge others without really thinking about it (based on clothes, gender, attractiveness, accent, race, politics, age)?

Think of some instances when you've judged another person's actions based on your own experience, rather than theirs. Can you recall instances when you were judged, not on what happened but on what someone else assumed *must* have happened, based on their experience? Elaborate on these situations and your response to them.

How might a loving person who believes in God respect the beliefs of a loving person who does not? And how might a loving person who does not believe in God respect the beliefs of a loving person who does?

8

What Does It Mean to Practice Interfaith?

I went to an "Interfaith Dinner" not long ago. There, one of the speakers told the audience that "Christianity is more than a religion; it is a way of life." Each speaker, from each of the differing faiths represented at that dinner, agreed that their spiritual path, too, was more than a religion; it was also a way of life. I feel certain that people from the many spiritual paths not represented at that dinner would have said something similar.

Each of our spiritual paths, if practiced in day-to-day living, would lead to remarkably similar lives, filled with love, compassion, and community. Yet most of us don't lead these kinds of lives. Interfaith, as a faith, reminds us that it is not the spiritual path we follow, but how we follow that path that truly matters.

Yes, all of our spiritual paths can be guides to a compassionate and loving life. But the question stubbornly remains: Do we actually live that way of life or do we merely profess it and move on? The truth of it is, it is so much easier to profess love than to live it. Interfaith, as a faith, asks us to live our faith and to worry much, much less about how we profess it.

Thus, to be a good Interfaither is to be a good Christian, or a good Jew, or a good Baha'i, Buddhist, Muslim, or Humanist. It is to be a good human being: loving, compassionate, and in community with our human family.

That said, if an Interfaither is a person who embraces Interfaith as a faith and practices Interfaith in his or her daily life, the question is not "What would that look like?" We already know that, if practiced, it would be a life of compassion, love, and action in community. The question, therefore, is this: "How?" How do we actually get there? This brings us back to the essence of this book: *practical* Interfaith. What are some particularly Interfaith ways that might help guide us to our goal of love, compassion, and community?

President Ronald Reagan famously said in a speech at the Brandenburg Gate and the wall that divided East and West Berlin, "Mr. Gorbachev, Mr. Gorbachev, open this gate. Mr. Gorbachev, tear down this wall."[1]

We all need to open the gates of love, compassion, and community. We need to tear down the walls that divide us. So easily said. But our walls of division have stood so very high for so very long. How can we possibly tear them down? I believe that the answer is that they must be torn down brick by brick. This means that we are not going to tear these walls down in a day, a week, or a year. We have to think longer term than that. We have to think of our children and their children. Our love and compassion must extend generationally forward.

But while it will indeed take time as well as intent, we can still make a start. With a nod to the first-century BCE Jewish rabbi and sage Hillel, if we don't, who will? If not now, when? Indeed, one of the most important ways we can practice our Interfaith is by moving with intention to begin to remove the bricks that make that wall of human division—and subdivision—so formidable.

So what are some of the bricks comprising those walls of division that we might begin to tear down? I would like to start with two. These bricks are by no means the sole cause of our divisions. But they are foundational, and I believe the wall of division they support depends on them. So in terms of beginning to live our Interfaith, they are an essential place to start. If we can begin to address these bricks, we will indeed be practicing Interfaith—and living it.

Our Conversational Bricks

The following two foundational bricks support a wall of division that continues to keep us from having a truly helpful dialogue with one another. They help to keep our souls imprisoned by divisions into "them" and "us."

These bricks come first because, frankly, if we can't even discuss our divisions, the walls that separate us will remain. While they won't be easy to dislodge, these are, I believe, among the most basic of the bricks we need to send back to the brickyard.

The First Brick: Anyone Who Disagrees with Me Is Evil

This foundational brick is a disquietingly tried and much too true way of making any substantive conversation all but impossible. Our various spiritual paths have cowered behind it on and off for millennia. But it's not just about the sacred. Listen, if you dare, to what passes for political discourse today. Anyone who disagrees with another's politics is not merely wrong or misguided, but out to destroy God and country.

We need to recognize that it's not just "them." It's not just "those people." It's "us" as well. Unless we are very aware and intentional, it is almost impossible for any of us not to get caught up in demonizing the "other." Indeed, the very act of creating the "other" is the essence of demonizing. Creating the "other" makes anyone who disagrees with us not really human and certainly not worthy of respect. "We're rational. But those people. *Those people*. You just can't reason with them." Sound familiar?

OK. So how do we begin the process of brick removal? We need to focus first on ourselves. We need to stop demonizing those we disagree with and those who disagree with us. We also need to start naming the very process of demonizing every time we hear it. Whether it comes from the left or the right, whether it comes from those who follow our spiritual path, another path, or no path, we need to name demonization when we hear it ... and when we read it in the paper. Only when enough of us stop demonizing others and name demonizing for what it is will we ever start making demonizing the "other" the moral embarrassment it ought to be. Moreover, the two actions must be linked. Naming demonization while we practice it ourselves is a pointless exercise. But quietly eliminating demonization from our own repertoire while not at the same time pointing out with clarity and conviction when it is used by others is, in effect, unilateral disarmament and rather toxic.

First Brick Removal

1. We want to listen for words like "those people" in our own conversation and remind ourselves that "those people" are no more or

less human than we are. We are all brothers and sisters. This does not mean that we won't disagree, become upset, or even become furious with each other from time to time. But, at the end of the day, "those people" are a part of "us." We need to listen to others as we would wish to be listened to. This doesn't happen overnight. But becoming aware is our important first step.

2. We want to begin to speak up when we hear a group being demonized, especially when we don't agree with the group. As example, if we are Democrats speaking with other Democrats, and someone demonizes Republicans, we want to point out what's happening. This does not mean that, as a Democrat, we agree with the Republican point being discussed but rather we're recognizing that Republicans are human beings, too. And the same holds true for Republicans speaking with other Republicans about Democrats. It also holds true for Christians talking about Muslims. The bottom line is that we don't have to agree with each other to be respectful. But we do have to be respectful if we hope to make any real progress.

The Second Brick: I Don't Have to Listen to You; I Know What You're Going to Say

This conversation-stopper is blood brother (sister) to demonizing. After all, who needs to listen to a demon? It is the simplest and possibly the most effective way of never having to think. "I don't have to listen. I know what I know. I know what's right. End of conversation."

Even if we don't say this aloud, much too often, unless we are exceedingly careful, all of us tend to hear what we expect to hear, whether it's actually said or not. Listening, truly listening, has all but become a lost art. I believe a large reason for this is because in no small part listening has become a lost virtue. I believe that we need to start thinking of the very act of listening as something both important and positive—a virtue to be practiced.

Truly listening is much more than simply not speaking. If I am truly listening, I am engaged in what you are saying. I'm not thinking about tomorrow's to-do list or trying to come up with three reasons why I think you are wrong. If I'm truly listening, I'm seeking to understand both what you are saying and why.

More than that, if we are honest, we will recognize that most of us only half-listen to the other person at best. We're keeping in mind how we will respond. I would suggest the modestly revolutionary idea that if we are listening to someone and don't, with some frequency, actually lose our own train of thought, then we aren't really listening. True listening is not a matter of hearing enough to come up with a rebuttal. It's putting aside our preconceived notions of what we are so very certain the person is saying, or is about to say, and actually hearing what is being said. If we ask questions, we are asking for clarification of something we don't understand, rather than our more common habit of automatically challenging another person's point of view.

Not that we won't disagree with each other. Being human, we are going to disagree. But let us at least strive to disagree with what is actually said rather than some preconceived notion. And let us agree to disagree respectfully.

There appears to be a rather strange disease rampant these days. The disease manifests itself in the belief that anyone who disagrees with us is challenging our personhood. This disease, a pandemic in our politics as well as along our spiritual pathways, contributes mightily to making listening to another person's point of view all but impossible. If I accept the notion that any movement from my core beliefs dehumanizes me, then I can't afford to give an inch. Moreover, implicit in that argument is the idea that anyone who disagrees with me isn't just plain wrong but a threat to my beliefs and to my sense of myself. Thus the simple act of listening becomes a true act of courage.

Many seminaries try to teach listening. I say "try" because listening and learning to listen are hard work. It is deeply spiritual work as well, because the very first thing to understand about listening is that it requires us to treat the person we are listening to with respect, and to embrace that person's humanity in our heart. So truly listening to another person is a spiritual act.

How do we begin to dislodge this second brick of division? The bottom line is respect. We need to try to understand why a person feels the way he or she does. We can't do that if we won't respect the other person's humanity. Let's be clear here. This doesn't mean that if we just respect each other we'll all agree. To expect that is foolish. Respecting each other won't solve our problems or bring about world peace. It is a start, only a first step, on our way to truly and compassionately listening to one another. But it is a crucial first step if we truly hope some day to demolish the walls that keep us both divided and at each other's throats.

Second Brick Removal

1. We want to remind ourselves that listening is both an act of courage and a virtue. Like most virtues, it doesn't come without practice and effort. That's why listening takes courage. So the first act of brick removal is to practice listening. The best place to start is with friends. We want to relearn the art of listening, for the art of listening has been all but drummed out of us.

   This will take time. We want and need to acknowledge that. This is one well-entrenched brick. Dislodging it may be as difficult or more difficult than giving up smoking!

2. After listening, the question must not be, Do I agree or disagree? The two questions we want to be able to answer after listening to someone is, first, Do we understand what they've said? (If not, we need to ask questions.) And, second, Do we understand why they believe what they've said? (If not, again, we need to ask questions.) What we need to learn, and practice, and remember is that the question, Do I agree or disagree? is not part of listening. The question "Do I agree?" comes only after we understand both what a person has actually said and why he or she has said it.

Fear: Brick Removal's Silent Foe

As we conclude this chapter, it's worth emphasizing that our spiritual paths all remind us of the need not only for love and compassion but also for community. The three are interwoven. Our love and compassion become meaningless if they are merely self-directed. And there can be no community without love and compassion.

Drawing from the writings of Baha'u'llah, the Baha'i tell us, "O contending peoples and kindreds of the earth! Set your faces toward unity and let the radiance of its light shine upon you."[2]

In their sacred scripture, *Adi Granth,* the Sikhs are more succinct: "Let all humanity be thy sect."[3]

From Hebrew Scripture, "For My house shall be called a house of prayer for all peoples" (Isaiah 56:7).

My personal favorite comes from a Nigerian proverb, "When one finger is sore you do not cut it off."[4]

With such eloquent unanimity, what's the problem? The problem is us. We humans are a small and fear-filled race. Many, if not most of our bricks of division have at the very least a component that can be traced to fear. Much too frequently we fear not having enough and then, once we have what we need, we fear losing it. But perhaps the most potent and spiritually debilitating fear is the fear of the "other," someone "not like us." Indeed, one of the most powerful positions to be in is to be able to decide who is "them" and who is "us."

Science fiction author Frank Herbert, in his novel *Dune,* puts it well: "I must not fear. Fear is the mind-killer. Fear is the little-death that leads to total obliteration."[5]

But only the dead are fearless. Because we are fearful by nature—whether we choose to admit it or not—it would be both foolish and rather pointless to say, "Well, stop it!"[6] What is important is to recognize our fears, name them, and not allow ourselves to be ruled by them.

So how do we accomplish this minor miracle? There are two hugely important components. The first is to acknowledge and recognize our fears. It's important for us to ask ourselves, What am I afraid of? We need to ask, What truly scares me about others? Is it people who are different? Is it the spiritual paths that are different? A lifestyle that is different? Recognizing our fears doesn't mean we'll banish them. But if we can at least recognize what truly scares us, we are on the right track toward managing them.

Perhaps even more important, if we recognize our fears, we can become aware when someone is trying to play on our fears to manipulate us. The truth of it is, the person who tells us to be afraid seeks to enslave us. Keeping us fearful of others is how many people make their living, and how others make themselves exceedingly powerful. It is an axiom as old as the very first dictator: If you want to control a people, first make them afraid.

To be free is not to be fearless but, rather, to acknowledge our fears and not allow ourselves to be ruled by them. Only if we are free can we begin the crucially important task of brick removal. It's going to take time. We are definitely going to need to practice our Interfaith.

A Bit Deeper

Questions for Discussion

How do you tend to refer to people whose politics falls on the other side of the political spectrum from yours (left or right)? If you say "them" or "those people," what do you mean by that?

Listen for demonizing of "others." How might you be able to express strong disagreement without demonizing?

Has anyone ever been so "sure" he or she knows what you're going to say that you never have the chance to actually express yourself? When did that happen? How did it make you feel?

Can you name some of your most basic fears (poverty, disease, being hurt, being homeless, being alone)? Having named your fears, how might you acknowledge that they are there without being ruled by them?

If you are in a group, practice listening, always keeping in mind that what you need to answer after listening is not "Do I agree or disagree?" but rather "Do I understand both what the person is saying and why?" Where do you feel your listening strengths lie? Where might you need some work?

9

THE FOUNDATION OF INTERFAITH DIALOGUE

O K. We want to practice Interfaith. We've done some brick removal, or at least we're working on it. So how do we take Interfaith out of the theoretical and truly make it part of our lives? I believe the best place to start is with interfaith dialogue. This is why our conversational bricks were singled out as the first ones to deal with.

It's important to acknowledge that not everyone will have the same interfaith goal. For some of us, dialogue can be a foundational first step toward the goal of an Interfaith church, where people of differing spiritual paths come together regularly to pray together and feel inspired, rather than threatened by our marvelously diverse spiritual journeys. For others of us, the goal may be simpler—no less important, but simpler—namely, to create a community where interfaith conversation can be nurtured, no congregation involved, where we can dial down the level of mistrust and be able to appreciate the sacred within us all.

As noted before, an Interfaith church builds on the foundation of Interfaith as a faith that embraces humanity's diverse paths to approaching the sacred, as long as those paths are rooted in love, compassion, and community. Interfaith dialogue does not necessarily embrace Interfaith as a faith. Rather, it brings people of differing spiritual paths together for respectful talk. Both an Interfaith church and interfaith dialogue are valuable and significant. Still, it is important to understand that they are not the same.

Nevertheless, as I've worked with both interfaith and Interfaith goals, I've come to believe that an Interfaith church and interfaith dialogue both have the same starting point: compassionate, respectful conversation. But what does such an interfaith conversation entail and, with so much dividing us, how do we get there?

A Very Short History of Interfaith Dialogue

Interfaith dialogue has a rather lengthy and, truth be told, sordid history, founded on the belief that there is only one right approach to the sacred. As we've seen, for a very long time, the epitome of interfaith dialogue has been "I'm right, and you're going to hell. Let's talk!" When conversation was pursued past that opening salvo, what the unfortunate target of the interfaith dialogue was likely to hear was something like this: "But don't be afraid. I'm lovingly patient. I'm more than willing to talk as long as necessary ... until you agree with me and realize that I'm right." This is how most people have experienced interfaith dialogue and why so many still shy away from it.

The initial Parliament of the World's Religions in 1893 in Chicago was perhaps the first large-scale, if somewhat tentative, step away from this model of dialogue. It was part of the World Columbian Exposition—an early world's fair—and while some groups, such as the Sikhs and those following most indigenous spiritual paths, were not included, this coming together to explore differing religions was certainly a historic first. Over time there have been numerous other steps as well. Nonetheless, it's worth noting that genuine interfaith dialogue remains rare for the simple reason that so many of us still cling to the toxic idea that one spiritual path has a lock on the truth about the sacred.

It's important to acknowledge this, but not because interfaith dialogue is impossible. Interfaith dialogue is indeed difficult, but we humans tackle the difficult all the time. What we do need to discard are any leftover rose-tinted glasses that happen to be lying around the house. If we enter into interfaith dialogue unprepared—and in the past far too many of us have—we will most likely end up as so many of our predecessors have: disappointed and perhaps disillusioned. We want to acknowledge the challenge of interfaith dialogue, not because we want to avoid it but because we want to be prepared to meet that challenge and stare it down.

Beginning an Authentic Interfaith Dialogue

How do we begin an authentic interfaith dialogue? In a word—slowly. Think of building a successful interfaith dialogue like building a house. If, in our eagerness to get going, we simply throw up some walls, our house won't stand. It needs a foundation. As with a house, to build an interfaith dialogue of value, step 1 is to establish a secure foundation.

Many of us may well respond, "We already know how to discuss things! Good grief, we don't need to practice." But, with all due respect, we *do* need to practice. We are much too used to arguing about our faith-paths, debating who we believe is right. Some of us who consider ourselves tolerant are used to thinking of other faith-paths as exotic, or quaint, and that's not the same as having a dialogue. All of us have some bad and ingrained habits that we need to address if we hope to make our dialogue a positive experience.

There may come a time, and I would love to live long enough to see it, that interfaith dialogue becomes the norm. There may come a time when people of all faiths have learned to discuss their faith without being aggressive or defensive, when talking about their spiritual path carries no hidden agenda or fear. But we need to understand that today is not yet that time. So when we talk about starting an authentic interfaith dialogue, we need to start with some very basic building blocks.

It's important to pause here. What do I mean by "authentic" interfaith dialogue? Am I suggesting that people must believe in Interfaith before they can enter into an interfaith dialogue? The answer is emphatically *no*. We seek a benchmark, not dogma. Authentic interfaith dialogue describes the nature of the conversation, not the beliefs of the participants.

That's the essence of it. Dialogue is not debate; it is not about converting or convincing another. Nor is it about defending our own faith or spiritual path from someone else's attempt to convert or convince. It may sound self-evident, but it is also worth noting that by definition, a dialogue is not a monologue. A dialogue cannot just be me speaking endlessly until you understand. I must want to understand your spiritual path as much as you want to understand mine. More than that, for interfaith dialogue to be authentic, it needs to be a respectful sharing of our spiritual selves. The purpose of interfaith dialogue then is not to determine who is right, but to better understand the spiritual path of a fellow human being.

As example, not long ago I had an interfaith dialogue with a member of the local Ahmadiyya Muslim community. He shared with me his belief that Islam is the focal point of God and that the Ahmadiyya movement is the truest form of Islam. We talked over coffee for over an hour. My new friend did not change his beliefs and, importantly, he did not try to change mine. Rather he shared his beliefs and I shared mine, and we shared our rather different beliefs respectfully. We never argued. When we were done, I had a better idea of what he believed—though one hour is hardly sufficient to grasp anything particularly deep—and he had a better idea of what I believed. We didn't try to change the other; rather, we tried to understand each other. We respected our common humanity. That is an interfaith dialogue, albeit a short one.

But, for many of us, to share without proselytizing, to listen without feeling the need to argue, to ask questions of one another only for clarification rather than to challenge—particularly when it comes to issues of faith—these are new skills. So let's start at the beginning.

A Circle of Trust

Whether your purpose is to stay with interfaith dialogue or at some point to start an Interfaith church, to succeed I believe you'll need to create what renowned author and spiritual teacher Parker J. Palmer calls a "circle of trust."[1] Without trust, without what I tend to refer to as "safe space," it is immensely difficult, if not impossible, to engage in real dialogue.

In the beginning, what you'll want to do together with your new circle is create safe, sacred space for one another. Even among friends, this may take time. Let it. Trust doesn't come easily. As you create safe space, your circle of trust, you'll share with each other your spiritual paths, recognizing that this may well be a learning process for you as well as your friends. Once the circle is strong, and the nature of safe space understood, it is time to broaden the circle. But, for now, keep the circle small, and common reading is a good place to start.[2]

How small? I would urge you to form your first circle of trust with at least two or three and probably no more than five like-minded people, even if they are of the same spiritual path, though it is certainly preferable if they are from different paths or at the least from differing branches of the same path (Catholic and Methodist, as an example, or Sunni and Shi'a). In starting with these few like-minded people, you'll build a solid core, to discern and be able to articulate a common purpose. It also helps to allow some time for much-needed practice in the art of creating safe, sacred space.

One way to establish trust within the circle, to protect the safety of the space, is to have a few agreed-upon understandings before you begin. In *A Hidden Wholeness,* Parker J. Palmer goes into this at length, but I believe one essential ingredient is to establish a covenant that what is said in the room stays there. Among other things it means that things revealed in the room aren't discussed, even in friendship, outside the room.

In addition, all involved need to agree that trying to persuade another about the rightness of his or her spiritual path is off the table. Indeed, I would urge folks to begin each get-together saying aloud and in unison: "We agree that we are here to listen and to share, not to convert or convince. We covenant to respect each other's beliefs, and when we ask questions concerning our faiths, we will ask only for clarification and never to challenge." This is crucial in creating safe, sacred space.

When your small group feels comfortable, I would encourage you to undertake a wonderful, soul-filling spiritual exercise. It's not something I invented. It is something I was introduced to years ago and that I have borrowed and used with great success several times since.

First comes some homework. At least a week before the discussion, every person who will be involved needs to do some self-exploration. Ask participants—including, of course, yourself—to think about their spiritual journey, where they are now and where they were spiritually as far back into their childhood as they can remember. What events called to them, influenced them, moved them—as a child, as an adolescent, as an adult? Then ask them to chart their spiritual journey from childhood to the present. Some people may want to use a graph. Others might chart a road that leads this way or that. Some people may want to draw something, perhaps a tree with their spiritual experiences as branches—always keeping in mind that this is not an art class and no one is expected to be a Rembrandt. What were the bumps, the high points, the changes of direction, the moments and people of influence—positive and negative—along their spiritual journey? The idea is for people to challenge themselves as they ponder and remember their spiritual journey.

It is important to make a physical representation of your journey and not rely on memory or simply words. As you do, things you've long since forgotten will suddenly pop into your mind. Creating this physical representation of your spiritual journey is itself a spiritual journey.

The next step in the exercise is to share your physical representations with the rest of the circle. As you listen to each other's spiritual journeys, it's important to ask questions only for clarification. You're not gathered to judge or challenge one another, but to share. Like creating the physical manifestation of your spiritual journey, sharing it is another wonderful and sometimes surprising journey as well.

There are, of course, whole books on dialogue. This is but a start. Enjoy. Authentic interfaith dialogue becomes a wonderful affirmation of the diversity of the human spirit. One potential side benefit is that learning to listen to one another tends to spill out into our lives as a whole. Truly listening to the other person, and taking pains to hear what is actually said, becomes a positive and enriching part of our lives.

Interfaith dialogue is becoming more than simply a goal but an attainable, important goal. But what if we want to go further than this? What if we want to come together, not just once in a while, but regularly? What if we want to come together to share our spiritual paths in sacred space, not to convert each other or to try to discern whose path is right, but because we truly want to learn about each other?

Is there a way to come together, to share sacred space, and to learn about each other without cutting our ties to our own sacred path? Yes, there is. It's called an Interfaith church and at the Living Interfaith Church, we've achieved it. It works. In Part III, "Starting an Interfaith Church," we'll examine some of the bumps as well as the highs we have experienced along the way.

Yet, while I strongly believe in the healing power of coming together in sacred space to share and celebrate our spiritual diversity, that isn't the only reason for interfaith dialogue.

While some of us may indeed dream of starting an Interfaith congregation, others may think of an Interfaith congregation as a nice idea, but their goal is to build a community where interfaith dialogue can be nurtured. Both of these approaches are worthwhile, important, and deserve exploring. We must keep in mind, however, that, whatever our goal, our first step is successful interfaith dialogue.

A Bit Deeper

Questions for Discussion

Take some time and make a graphic representation of your own spiritual journey, from your earliest memory to the present. What surprises you? What had you forgotten or "misplaced"?

Practice the art of asking for clarification, rather than offering arguments. Repeat back (that is, mirror) the essence of what you've been told, remembering that the goal is to be able to answer, "What did s/he say, and what were the reasons/feelings/beliefs behind what was said?" and *not* "Do I agree or disagree?"

10

BROADENING THE DIALOGUE

Once your small circle is strong, and comfortable with the covenants and care that make a true dialogue possible—which will likely take several months—it may be time to broaden the circle. As you do, it's important to remember that many people have experienced an invitation to share as "Let's have a dialogue, and we'll keep talking until you realize that I'm right." Given this rather arrogant and unfortunate history of interfaith dialogue, you need to be careful and clear about your intent for true dialogue.

Perhaps the easiest way to begin to broaden the dialogue is as a reading group—reading a text and then discussing how each person relates to it. See the Suggestions for Further Reading section of this book for some recommendations. With your initial core group having already read some of the books, they can serve as helpful guides as your new, broader group begins to work together.

Here are some questions to start with as you discuss each book:

"What challenges you in the text?"

"How does this apply to your life experience?"

Again, what is crucial is to engage in an honest, safe sharing. We are not looking for "I agree" or "I disagree." Rather, we are looking for "I feel" and "How do you feel?"

Once everyone feels comfortable, I'd again strongly suggest sharing your spiritual journeys with one another. You may have already shared this with the core group earlier, but every time we consider our journeys we not only learn more about each other, but we also learn more about ourselves. Some things that may not have occurred to us the first time we thought about our spiritual journey will now seem important and obvious.

But How Do We Find People?

More than once I've been asked, "How do we start? Where do we find people?" Good questions! No one size fits all. But assuming you've taken the time to build a small core group, here are some ways to broaden the discussion. Keep in mind, however, that these suggestions are not likely to work well unless you live in or near at least a medium-sized city.

Meetup

You might want to check out Meetup.com. Meetup offers an affordable price to form and promote your interfaith discussion group (at present it's payable every six months). There is no charge for a person to join Meetup and check out groups. By all means, choose your own words, but the essence of your description on Meetup might be something like this: "We meet once a month to share our spiritual paths. We listen to and learn from each other. We gather neither to convert nor to convince but rather to experience and enjoy our profound spiritual diversity."

You are allowed to ask people who join your Meetup group to answer some questions. Here are three questions our group asks new Meetup members to answer:

1. Am I willing to share who I am and my spiritual path in an open and loving way without attempting to convert or convince?

2. Am I committed to hearing and respecting the spiritual paths of others without feeling pressured to convert or convince?

3. Am I open to our common humanity that recognizes differing spiritual paths without hierarchy?

In all honesty, the answers to the questions aren't all that important. It is the questions themselves, and the process of thinking about them, that help the newcomer understand that your group is intentional about creating safe space for a real dialogue.

Advertise in the Local Newspaper

This is cheaper out of the box, but much more expensive in the long run if you continue to run ads. Still, it might be a good way to announce your group. Here's a sample ad:

> **Interfaith Discussion:** Group forming to respectfully share our spiritual diversity with one another. All of goodwill, who come to share and to listen, NOT convert or convince, are welcome. 7:00 p.m. at XXX 1111 XYZ Street.

Where to Meet?

It might seem that someone's home would be ideal. But once you grow beyond your core group of a few people, I'd caution against that. While interfaith discussion tends to appeal to people who are genuinely interested in it, it can also bring out folks who have an agenda contrary to the group's goals. For that reason, I'd strongly suggest meeting in a public place.

Many pizza parlors and other restaurants have relatively small banquet rooms. You need to check, but, generally, if everyone who comes buys something, there's no charge for the room. And, let's face it, sharing food helps in sharing who we are.

Many churches, mosques, temples, synagogues, or other spiritual meeting centers are willing to let people use their space at times when they don't need it. If you tell them it's for interfaith discussion, some may be willing to let you use their facilities at no charge. Others will need to charge you something. So never assume. Always explore and ask.

Frequently, public libraries have rooms available for discussion groups. But again, check it out. Many—including the one nearest to where I live—do not allow food. Schools usually have rooms available on the weekends, but there's almost always a charge for the space.

Interfaith Exchanges

What about congregations that might want to enter into an interfaith dialogue with another congregation? As an example, say a Methodist church wants to enter into a dialogue with a nearby Jewish synagogue or a Muslim mosque. What then? I've never tried this, but I've always liked the idea. Here are some thoughts on how to do this. If you try them, let me know how it works out.

What I'd suggest is forming a small interfaith discussion group as described above with two to three members from each congregation participating. Again, safe, sacred space is always a primary concern and should be approached with intention. An intentional understanding that "We are not here to try to convert you, nor do we wish to be converted" will be crucial to your success.

Once the small group is successful in truly listening to one another and sharing rather than giving in to the temptation to try to convince, the group's members can report back to their respective congregations about what they've learned. At this point, a larger interfaith discussion group might be formed, with the smaller group once again acting as a foundation for supporting safe, sacred space.

Once the larger group is successful, the time has come for each spiritual community to invite the other to visit during an actual service, with a representative or two from the community—ideally these representatives will have participated in the interfaith discussions before—sitting with the visitors and acting as host. If this is done with respect and interfaith intention, it can provide a rich and truly rewarding experience of the sacred.

Interfaith dialogue can be hugely rewarding and can help to build important bridges between people and spiritual communities. But what I am personally committed to are Interfaith congregations. What is that about? And why do we call these congregations Interfaith churches? That takes us to Part III.

Voices of Interfaith

Patrick S. McKenna

By my late teens, I knew that my parents' strict Christian faith wasn't a good fit for me. I never felt the connection to the God and Jesus of the Bible that others seemed to (and I was supposed to) experience. However, I've always had a deep sense of my own spirituality; even during the eight or so years I left religion completely and considered myself an atheist, I still felt that I needed something more than just reason or rote to sustain me.

From my mid-teens, I was called to Neo-Paganism, earth-centered religion, although mine is a godless path. I am nourished and sustained by my connection to the natural world and the rhythms of the seasons. On my journey, I looked into other faith traditions, examining Buddhism, Islam, Hinduism, and others, and always came back to Paganism.

Over my lifetime, I've come to see religion as beautiful and necessary to humanity's search to understand ourselves as a species and the world around us. Interfaith is a way to experience that search that validates us all, whether we follow Abrahamic traditions, indigenous paths, personal spirituality, even Humanism. Living Interfaith Church is a way that allows me to celebrate the faiths and traditions of others while remaining firmly centered on my own path. There's no compromising or tepid tolerance. We come together to share our different spiritual lives and create a community of people building peace through real understanding.

Dilara Hafiz

I have been living and breathing interfaith from Day 1! Since my father is a Sunni Muslim and my mother is a Methodist Christian, I have been fortunate to have been exposed to both faiths since as long as I can remember. We celebrated both Christmas and the two Eids, but more than the cultural observances, my parents instilled in me a firm belief in God and the importance of morals and values that are common to both Islam and Christianity. Although I did not truly learn or understand the details of doctrinal beliefs of these two faiths until I was much older, I do feel that my early spiritual path was one of a belief in God, the Hereafter, and the accountability of self.

My interfaith upbringing grounded me firmly in open-mindedness and a willingness to listen to others' spiritual journeys. It was my my marriage to a Muslim and our joint desire to impart the basics of an Islamic education to our children that actually led to my own self-education in Islam. As I learned the Qur'an and the basics of Islamic history and practice alongside my children, I feel that I benefited from both the cultural background from my father as well as the intellectual inquiry of studying Islam, almost from a convert's perspective. I questioned *everything*! This desire to fully understand Islam led to my present situation where I feel totally comfortable as an informed, educated Muslim woman. In fact, it was the tragic events of 9/11 that propelled my family to write a book, *The American Muslim Teenager's Handbook,* as our attempt to reduce misconceptions about Islam in America.

Having been involved with interfaith on a professional basis for the past ten years, I have come full circle in my understanding of the oneness of humanity. If believers and nonbelievers, atheists and agnostics, conservative and liberals ... if *all* of us can affirm our connections to each other and our desire to serve our community and our world, then surely we can find common ground in celebrating this love. By joining a vibrant Living Interfaith community, I feel inspired to be the best Muslim I can be, free from the judgment of others who may subscribe to a narrow interpretation of my faith.

Part III

Starting an Interfaith Church

11

HOLDING SAFE, SACRED SPACE

Before considering the need for safe, sacred space to nurture Interfaith, there are some foundational questions to ask. We've already spoken about interfaith dialogue, and seen that it's both important and doable. So as we begin this section, the first question to ask is this: Is coming together to celebrate our diversity really all that important? Next we'll want to examine, What exactly do we mean by "safe, sacred space"? And, once again, we'll ask: Is it really all that important? Our last and perhaps most difficult question is this: If we decide that we want to come together to form a sacred community, why might we want to call our Interfaith congregation an Interfaith "church"?

Why Coming Together Matters

Particularly in our larger cities, there are more and more interfaith services popping up. Many if not most of these center around a holiday like Thanksgiving. These interfaith services can be beautiful and important. I would never argue that they shouldn't happen. But I'd suggest that coming together once or twice a year is not nearly often enough if we wish to practice Interfaith. Why? Well, imagine wanting to play in a band and practicing your instrument only once or twice a year!

Interfaith, as a faith, is new. It involves a paradigm shift that will take a lot of practice. The simple fact of it is that we'll need to come together, and regularly, if we sincerely want to become comfortable with our diversity. If we recognize that there are many roads to the top of our spiritual mountain, then it is important for us to explore our many paths. If we are to respect and honor our diverse paths, we also need to understand them better, and that will take time. We need to practice our Interfaith, not merely proclaim it.

But wait! Does that mean we need to leave our own spiritual path behind? Emphatically no! We'll explore this question more deeply later on, but, for now, what we need to understand is that the essence of Interfaith, as a faith, is a new paradigm of both/and rather than the old paradigm of either/or. Interfaith does not urge anyone to abandon his or her spiritual path. Rather, it teaches us that, as we walk our own path, it is valuable to be both aware and respectful of paths that differ from our own—as long as the goal of that path is love, compassion, and community. We make the effort to come together as a way of sharing our spiritual paths and as a reminder that such sharing takes practice.

There is another, even more practical, reason for coming together to practice our Interfaith. Muslims did not suddenly appear in the United States in 2001. There have been Muslim U.S. citizens from the very founding of the country. But Muslims, like Christians, Buddhists, Jews, and others, have tended to worship in their own communities. Few of us who weren't Muslim had even the most rudimentary understanding of the spiritual underpinnings of this profound and important spiritual path. Then came September 11, 2001, the World Trade Center and other terrorist attacks, and suddenly people became very aware of Islam. Yet Islam remained foreign to most of us, and history has shown over and over again that ignorance is the perfect incubator for bigotry.

Even now, some of us will still believe almost any weird thing we are told about Islam. Yes, there are some demagogues who willfully misrepresent the Muslim faith because they can make a buck—OK, actually huge piles of bucks. But the folks these demagogues make their money from are not evil. They are ignorant, and when we are ignorant it is so very easy to make us afraid. So many are willing to believe just about anything bad regarding Islam because they simply don't know any better, and their ignorance makes them easy targets for the fearmongers.

I have a particular sensitivity to this because, not that long ago, the same venom was directed against Jews. What is striking about much of the anti-Muslim rhetoric is that it is almost word for word the anti-Jewish rhetoric that I still remember from my childhood. This rhetoric was fueled by anti-Jewish demagogues, but most of the people who bought into the hate simply didn't know any better. They bought into the "World Zionist conspiracy" not out of hate but out of ignorance. Before I was born, Hitler galvanized Europe into the huge spasm of anti-Jewish fear that allowed the *Shoah* (Holocaust) to take place with minimal protest based on the self-same ignorance.

There are still ignorant people. But through Interfaith we can begin to address that ignorance, whether it's aimed at Muslims, Jews, Sikhs, Buddhists, Baha'i, or people of any other spiritual path.

Once we experience each others' faiths and spiritual paths, it becomes far more difficult to be fooled by the snake oil salesmen (-women) who seek to make a fortune off our ignorance and fear. But learning about another's spiritual pathway involves intention. We were told by our parents never to talk about religion in "polite company" for a reason. The paradigm of right belief remains strong. The paradigm of "We're right, and you're going to hell" remains strong. Thus, embracing the idea of Interfaith as a faith that honors and respects our diverse spiritual paths isn't enough. We also need to act, and this involves coming together in safe sacred space to practice Interfaith.

What Do We Mean by "Safe, Sacred Space"?

Keeping our sacred space safe means creating a space where all of us can be who we are without having to be on guard against in-your-face or more subtle attempts to convert us to a differing spiritual path. If our sacred space is safe, we won't feel the need to be defensive about our spiritual path, even and particularly if our path is different from another person's. "Safe space" also means that others don't have to be defensive when they share their spiritual selves with us. Within safe, sacred space, converting or convincing is off the table as a given. So is judging the rightness of another person's beliefs. We gather to share and to learn, as we work to build a just community of compassion and love.

Sounds simple enough, doesn't it? But it's neither simple nor easy—for we are tribal creatures by nature. As mentioned earlier, it will take ongoing intention to break free of our us-and-them tribalism. This is as true along our spiritual pathways as it is in our politics. Also, our tribalism isn't always something that is blatantly obvious. As example, there is a spiritual community I know of that prides itself in its proclamation that "All are welcome." So far so good. But we want to go one step further and ask, "All are welcome to do what?" "All are welcome to be what?"

There is, I believe, a profound difference between "All are welcome" to participate in "our" service, and "All are welcome to bring who they are into this shared space as part of us." Time to be clear. We are not speaking here of a difference between a right path and a wrong one. Both of these welcoming thoughts can be beautiful and valid. But they are different. The intent is different.

The metaphor of a salad bowl, not a melting pot, comes to mind. Sometimes a melting pot is seen as an ideal. No matter what our backgrounds, we all melt together to become one and the same. When I was growing up, the ideal of the United States as a melting pot was seen as a good thing. And a melting pot can still be a good thing. But it can also sometimes overwhelm the newcomer in favor of the old-timer. Perhaps more darkly, the melting pot metaphor may be used to idealize the majority and explicitly or, at best implicitly, signal to minorities that they are out of step. In essence, the darker side of the melting pot concept says to the outsider, Melt away your own identity and become like us. For me, a painful example of this comes at the beginning of the outstanding Spike Lee movie, *Malcolm X*. Before becoming radicalized, Malcolm tries very hard to blend in to white, European culture. He tries to be more "white," including submitting himself to the painful process of having his hair straightened. The tyranny of the melting pot is both evident and horrific.

The idea of the salad bowl is an acknowledgment that we're all in this together, but we still keep who we are intact. For me, as an Interfaither, this is progress. Yet I think we still need to be careful. I once gave a sermon on "The Revenge of the Croutons," which examined that if one part of our salad bowl considers itself superior to the rest of the salad, we approach George Orwell's *Animal Farm:* "All animals are equal. Some animals are more equal than others."

In Interfaith, we are not seeking a melting pot. We need to say this over and over, in a multitude of ways, because one of the most basic misunderstandings many people bring to the table is the thought that Interfaith melts—or seeks to melt—all spiritual paths into one. It does not. Interfaith does not ignore the fact that our spiritual paths are different and it doesn't seek to change that. What many of us seem to find difficult to imagine is the idea that we can respect our differences without denying or diminishing them.

This is the reason holding safe, sacred space is so critically important. Many people, including those of goodwill, are unable to find a way to wrap their minds around a respectful sharing of our diversity. Their minds and patterns of thinking only allow for a choice between a melting pot that eliminates all differences on the one hand, or one right belief that at best establishes a first among equals on the other. While Interfaith believes this way of thinking offers a very limited horizon, it is not to be taken lightly. A belief that we are faced with a choice of either/or has governed how humanity has approached our spiritual paths not just for centuries but for millennia. A change in our thinking and in our hearts that truly embraces our differences without hierarchy or melting pots constitutes a seismic shift in the very essence of our spiritual paradigm.

So we need not only to create safe, sacred space but also to be exceedingly intentional about it. This is one reason that, at the Living Interfaith Church, the opening of every service is the same. We repeat the welcome, not simply for any newcomers to our church but also as a reminder to each and every one of us, even if we have been coming for years. Safe, sacred space requires intention. This is how we begin our services:

> Welcome. Welcome to Living Interfaith. Know that the whole of you is welcome. You are not asked to leave who you are at the door. Bring who you are in with you. What you are asked to remember is that the people seated around you have brought who *they* are in through the door with them as well. And all, *all* of goodwill are welcome.

Goodwill and an active respect for our common humanity—these alone are the common denominators of our church.

Our church. Our *church*? Why, particularly with our call for a salad bowl approach to our spiritual paths, would we choose to use the word "church"? Doesn't "church" mean or at least imply Christian? How can we bring Jews, Muslims, Baha'i, Humanists, Buddhists, and others together in a "church"? These are good and important questions.

Why a "Church"?

There's no doubt that the word "church" is freighted with a lot of emo-
tion—both positive and negative. The words "church" and "Christian"
have become closely identified with each other. This being true, what is an
Interfaith congregation doing when it calls itself a church?

First, as is hopefully clear by now, there need be no orthodoxy involved.
The fact that Living Interfaith calls itself a church does not mean that other
Interfaith congregations need to follow. One possible option would be to
call our gathering the Living Interfaith Congregation. One Interfaith church
I know of and worked for has recently changed its name from Interfaith
Community Church to Interfaith Community Sanctuary. Why haven't we
followed suit?

We've discussed this very question more than once at our Helping
Hands—or board—meetings. We have stayed with "church," at least for
now, out of a desire to recapture what we believe may be the origins of the
Old English word "church"—namely, a sacred circle.[1] It is possible that, in
its oldest meaning, a church was a sacred circle. Over time, church became
the place where the sacred circle met. Yet it is certainly possible that a
sacred circle isn't the origin of "church." There is no way to know. Perhaps,
at some future time, we'll change our name to the Living Interfaith Circle,
or, as noted above, the Living Interfaith Congregation. But for now, we've
decided to stay with "church," with the idea of reclaiming "church" as a
more universal place of sacred gathering.

Whatever the words involved, why is the idea of a circle so important?
It is important to me, personally, because I have never been comfortable
with the idea of a spiritual leader—a rabbi, minister, priest, monk, imam,
or whatever—being anything other than a guide. I do not feel at all at ease
with thinking of spiritual leaders as having some kind of pipeline to the
divine and thus making proclamations of truth that are to be followed "or
else."[2] So the idea of a circle feels much more comfortable to me.

For many in our group, the idea of a sacred circle calls deeply to them.
Sacred circles have long been part of the human experience and they tran-
scend not only time but also cultures and continents. Circles reinforce the
"we." It's harder to demonize a "them" if we are all part of the same circle.

But being wedded to any one word can become an unfortunate first
step toward doctrine and dogma. The Interfaith theological framework of

love, compassion, and community that embraces our diversity with respect doesn't require the tyranny of exact replication. Indeed, it rejects that tyranny. So if people feel called to start an Interfaith spiritual community, whether they call it Living Interfaith or not, whether it is called an Interfaith church, an Interfaith circle, an Interfaith community, or something else, what we want to ensure is that the name we use has meaning to us.

What is important is that at the heart of whatever we call ourselves lies our salad bowl inclusivity—that we are open and inclusive of all of goodwill. Whatever we call ourselves, we seek to respect and honor our differences as we celebrate our common humanity. We embrace that we are indeed our brothers' and sisters' keepers. Our goal remains always to help those brothers and sisters who need our help without thoughts of "them" but always seeing only "us."

A Bit Deeper

Questions for Discussion

Share and explore what "safe, sacred space" means to you. How have you experienced sacred space that didn't feel safe?

Have you ever held a belief about a differing spiritual path, taught to you, perhaps, as a child, that you realized was untrue or unfounded when you met and got to know someone from that path? Explain.

How do you feel about the word "church" being used in an Interfaith context, meaning "circle." What does "church" mean to you? What are alternatives that resonate positively with you?

12

FOUNDATIONS FOR STARTING AN INTERFAITH SPIRITUAL COMMUNITY

They try very hard to teach you many things in seminary. Some of the lessons are profound and some are quite forgettable. One thing they make no attempt to teach is how to found a church, let alone how to start a new faith. So a lot of this has been "Make it up as you go." Much of this book, and particularly the chapters in this part, is being written in the hopes that the wheel of Interfaith won't have to keep being reinvented. Just as there any many spiritual paths that lead up the mountain, so there will be many paths to founding an Interfaith spiritual community. Here are some basics that may help.

What Do We Seek to Avoid?

As we begin to consider forming an Interfaith group, what are some things that we might well want to avoid? To put it succinctly, doctrine and dogma. From the beginning, as well as going forward, we need to keep in mind and heart that while what we believe is important, what truly counts is how we act. As practitioners of Interfaith, we want to be open and remain open to the many and diverse ways that may help us to act with love, compassion, and in community. For me, this means keeping four very important elements in mind.

1. Our beliefs are of value only if they help us to live a life of love, compassion, and in community. Whatever our spiritual path may be, if and when that path ceases to help us to be better human beings, we need to remember that it is only a path, and paths can be changed. Too often the sacred intent of our spiritual paths has gotten lost along the way because those paths calcified their guidelines into dogmatic absolutes. "The right way to experience the sacred is ..." We very much want to avoid that.

2. Because a particular spiritual path is helpful to me does not necessarily mean it will be helpful to you. Again, crucial to Interfaith is the avoidance of arranging our guidelines—our spiritual paths—into any kind of hierarchy. Our ways of getting to the mountaintop are going to vary. We must not let them divide us. We need to show right belief the door.[1]

3. To stay inclusive means resisting the temptation to carve things in stone. As example, there is nothing wrong with rituals. Rituals can be positive, helpful, and deeply comforting. Indeed, they can be inspiring and beautiful. But the moment a ritual becomes "This is the way we do it" instead of "This is a way we can do it," that ritual has become stonework and exclusionary.

4. While our differing paths may be profound and beautiful, they are not the same, and it is important to recognize and acknowledge that. Interfaith is about respecting and exploring our differences, not ignoring them.

It's always easier to list what not to do. Let's take a longer look at the positive side of things.

Forming a Spiritual Community

No community can exist without a foundational unifying common factor, though those factors may vary wildly. A common factor may be what is considered race, ethnicity, a spiritual path, or even a name.[2] For centuries, most of our spiritual communities have held to some form of right belief as their common ground. If we are to build a spiritual community that is not based on right belief, then what forms our common ground? For us, the tie that binds is our mutual respect for our diverse spiritual paths; we hold foremost in our minds that whatever our path and however we may walk it, that path must lead us to love, compassion, and community.

That's all well and good, but let's face it—it's not particularly helpful. How do we accomplish this daunting task? How do we build a new spiritual community based on love, compassion, and community? From my own experience, I would suggest that there are four essential elements.

1. Build a Core with a Common Understanding

Whenever I think of cores, I imagine apples. Consider: The core of an apple not only binds the apple together but also contains within it the seeds for new apple trees. That is impressive imagery. The core of a spiritual group should not only bind it together but always have within it the seeds of the future. Seeing our core in this way can help us avoid envisioning our core as some kind of keepers of the faith.

Having milked that metaphor about as far as we can, how do we build a solid, sustaining core group for a spiritual community? I believe that the key is to start small. Even if our vision is vast, we need to start small. A few chapters ago, we talked about starting a small interfaith discussion group. I believe that this is a great way to begin. Three, four, perhaps five people get together, learn about each other, and learn to trust one another. Without trust, there can be no sustainable core.

So where do we find the people for this core? There's no one answer. What is crucial is to talk about it. If you know a few people from differing spiritual paths, talk with them about it. If there happen to be any traditional interfaith dialogues taking place nearby, attend and talk about the idea of Interfaith as a faith. Also look for opportunities on social networking websites.

One good way to move forward with a small group of people is for everyone to read both *The Interfaith Alternative* and this book together and then to share thoughts about them. What does "Interfaith as a faith" mean? What does it ask of us? Frankly, as you talk about it, some may lose interest. That's OK and it's not personal! Others may become even more interested. In the meantime, as you talk, share your own spiritual experiences. Remember, you are not only building a core, you are also building a circle of trust.

Beyond the circle of trust, what is crucial in building a core is to build a common understanding. This does not in any way mean that everyone comes to an agreement about all things spiritual. What it does mean is that everyone comes to an agreement about what you will mean by "Interfaith" and also what you want to do about it, such as fostering interfaith dialogue, founding an Interfaith community that encourages dialogues and events, or founding an Interfaith congregation that meets regularly.

This may take time. That's OK. The astute reader may notice that a reminder to "Let it take time" is a much-repeated theme. One of the frustrating and, for me, rather foolish notions of our era is that we want everything and we want it now. I believe the best way to start is with our eyes on a very small, achievable goal, and to let it take whatever time is needed.

2. Build on Consensus

Building on consensus, rather than taking votes, may seem awkward and strange to many. But I believe in it, both as a philosophy of real inclusion and as a good way to build community. Building on consensus requires all involved to listen to each other and respect each other's opinions and concerns. It requires genuine—not grudging—compromise with real goodwill behind it. Building on consensus means, "OK, this is important to you, and that is important to me. How can we address both of our concerns? Why are these things important to us?" Once we understand why something is important to us, it becomes far more possible to address the concern.

Once again, this is why safe, sacred space and a circle of trust are so important. It is much easier to compromise when we trust the good intentions of the person we disagree with. It is virtually impossible to compromise when we don't.

3. Become Involved in the Larger Community

I believe a spiritual community that is concerned only with itself will, by its very nature, become increasingly isolated and dogmatic. It fosters the "us" and "them" way of looking at the world that can be so toxic. Thus, from the beginning seeking a way to be of help to our fellow humans by reaching out to the larger community serves both the group's self-interest and its altruistic mission.

Each community must answer for itself where and how it would like to participate in the larger community. It might be in preserving the environment, helping the hungry or the homeless, or serving seniors. My one suggestion would be that, in starting out, it is probably best to try to do one thing successfully rather than lurching from one cause to another. There are many ways to serve and so many needs. But the odds are you'll be small in numbers and resources at first. So pick one thing and go for it.

4. Commit to Keeping the Core Open

In my career as a choir director, serving different churches as well as temples and synagogues, I've far too often seen a core of committed individuals who have worked with each other for years, who know and like each other. But this very closeness can make it difficult for a new person to fit in. The core becomes a clique. I believe the only way to avoid this, if it can be avoided, is to understand the danger from the very beginning and to be intentional about keeping the core open and inviting to newcomers. One simple way to do this is to be intentional in welcoming and engaging in conversation not only first-timers but also people who come a second time as well.

It all goes back to intent. It's a matter of conscious action. Particularly in dealing with Interfaith, where the very idea is the welcoming of people of differing spiritual paths, I believe it is essential for us to realize that without intent behind our actions, the natural tendency is to develop "in" groups.

All of this seems terribly theoretical. So the question becomes: How were these ideas put into place to create the Living Interfaith Church?

A Bit Deeper

Questions for Discussion

Thinking of your own spiritual path, what are some examples of doctrine and dogma that may get in the way of the very reason for the doctrine in the first place?

List some rituals from your own spiritual path that have been of value to you. Why do you think they've been of comfort or helpful? How may they perhaps have held you back from growing spiritually?

Have you ever worked with others under a consensus model? If so, how has it felt? What worked for you? What did you find difficult?

Reflecting on your local community, where are there needs that may be the focus of your Interfaith community?

13

THE ROAD TO LIVING INTERFAITH

In the previous chapter we attempted to lay out some basics for forming an Interfaith spiritual community. But was it just a pleasant theory? How would it actually work? The happy answer is that Living Interfaith is based on the fundamentals of the previous chapter. So how did we do it? This chapter will chart how Living Interfaith got going. It's a personal journey, so by definition it will be a rather more personal chapter than the other chapters of *Practical Interfaith*.

Our foundational documents, as well as some readings and liturgy, can be found in the Resources for an Interfaith Community, beginning on page 101. What I'd like to chronicle here is how we got to where we are; how we started the Living Interfaith Church. My intent and hope are not to establish the right way of going forward. Rather, I want to share our experiences so that those who choose to follow may learn from them. This might well include thoughts of "Well, we certainly do *not* want to do that!" as well as, I hope, "That's cool. Let's try it."

Beginnings

No, I did not wake up one morning and decide, "Gee, wouldn't it be fun to start a church?" In truth, it was a long, zigzagging path. What's relevant is that I was working on the book that would become *The Interfaith Alternative* and had been for several years. The book called for people to come together and celebrate rather than be divided by their spiritual diversity.

But clearly, such a coming together was easier to say than to do. Was there even a chance that it could it be done?

Over the years, I learned there was an interfaith movement beginning to take root and to grow. This was and is a wonderfully positive step. Yet it seemed to me to fall short. I felt that interfaith as practiced was like two neighbors with a spiritual wall between them. Peering over the wall, they realized that just because a wall separated them, it did not mean they needed to or should throw rocks at each other. Perhaps once or twice a year, one neighbor would ask the other over for dinner.

I don't want to sell it short. This way of practicing interfaith was and is a significant and very positive step in the direction of recognizing our common humanity. But this approach to interfaith seemed to be the goal, the top of our mountain, if you will.

As I finished a draft of *The Interfaith Alternative,* I realized that my hope was that we would climb a bit higher. What I sought, to continue the analogy, was for neighbors to get together to share a meal at least once or twice a month. If neighbors could see each other regularly, share a meal and the joy of learning what's happening in their lives with intentional regularity, perhaps they could actually get to know one another. That's what I hoped for and that's the kind of spiritual community I had long dreamed of joining. Surely, I thought, it is time for us to come together, respecting our differences, indeed celebrating those differences, rather than being divided by them.[1]

But could people of goodwill come together? The idea of forming the Living Interfaith Church took shape as an attempt to show that this was not just a dream. It could be made real. Or could it? Interfaith, as a faith, was new. We were going to have to prove ourselves.

The Basics

The first step was to act on my understanding that this needed to be a "we" rather than a "me" project. I had interned for a year at the Interfaith Community Church—now Interfaith Community Sanctuary—in north Seattle. I was then ordained there and served for three wonderful and truly fulfilling years as an associate minister. The Interfaith Community Church (ICC) was filled with people I like, indeed love, and also respect. So why did I leave?

I'd raised the question of Interfaith as a faith with one of the lead ministers there and was informed firmly that ICC did not and would not embrace Interfaith as a faith. There were three lead ministers, and together they had formed ICC. I was an associate minister and very much the new kid on the block. It would have been both arrogant and out of place for me to argue. But I did and do feel deeply that Interfaith, as a faith, is an important way to move humanity toward a much-needed spiritual reconciliation. What was left was for me to start my own church. But one of the important things I took with me from my time at the Interfaith Community Church was the example of its commitment to working by consensus. That really felt like home.

While serving at ICC, I met Steve Crawford. Steve is a deep thinker about matters spiritual, and is deeply committed to all of humanity as brothers and sisters. When I talked to Steve about helping me start Living Interfaith, he agreed, though—and this is beautifully significant to remember—he never left ICC. He now splits his time between both churches. Since Steve was an important part of starting Living Interfaith, I've asked him to share some of his thoughts about the process. They appear on page 88.

While at ICC, I attended several annual interfaith conferences at a delightful and rustic spot called Camp Brotherhood. At one of those annual conferences I met Dilara Hafiz. Dilara is a human dynamo, who authored with her two teenage children *The American Muslim Teenager's Handbook*. Dilara is also deeply committed to reconciliation between our diverse spiritual paths and the brotherhood and sisterhood of all humanity. When I talked to her about helping me start Living Interfaith, she also agreed. What blew me away was that she knew when she agreed to help that she and her husband would need to leave for the Middle East in a year. Even so, Dilara committed to driving an hour in each direction to meet monthly with Steve, me, and others to figure out just how to start our new church. I've asked Dilara to share some of her thoughts about the process, and they appear on page 85.

But I had in my head a magic number of five. I wanted at least four people to work with me to create Living Interfaith. At a Camp Brotherhood conference, I announced my intention to start an Interfaith church, based on Interfaith as a faith, and asked for help. Two women came to talk with me about it and volunteered. But one never came to a meeting and the other came only to the first meeting.

Along the way I asked other people to join us as well but those connections didn't fall into place, either. So while I'd started with the idea of working with five of us, there were only three. This takes us to what I believe to be an essential lesson in starting a church or perhaps any venture ... namely, adapt, adapt, adapt. Steve, Dilara, and I decided that three would be a perfect number and we pressed ahead.

So what did we do? In preparation, I had read Parker Palmer's book *A Hidden Wholeness*. This is not a book about how to start a church, but I believed then and still believe that Palmer's thoughts on building a circle of trust are absolutely critical. I had intended to suggest that Steve and Dilara also read it, but after our first discussion I adapted again. They had enough to do. It became clear to me that, as long as I was intentional about building a circle of trust, that was all that was needed. I did ask Steve and Dilara to read the latest draft of what would become *The Interfaith Alternative*. The three of us needed to be on the same page in our thinking about what we were trying to establish.

The first few meetings focused on learning about each other, becoming comfortable with each other, and learning to trust one another. It quickly became apparent that Steve and Dilara wanted to move a whole lot faster than I had intended or was comfortable with. I wanted us to have a year to talk and carefully pull things together. My intent was to have discussions from September 2009 to August 2010, with September 2010 as the target date for our first service. But by January 2010, Steve and Dilara were both pushing to move our starting date up. To be honest, this was way out of my comfort zone, and I was scared out of my gourd. I didn't want to do it. But I knew that once again I needed to adapt.

At a meeting early that year, Rev. Heidi Fish, a friend of Dilara's, joined us. As I recall, Heidi is a Lutheran minister. I don't remember the reason Dilara brought her, but I remain eternally grateful that she did. I had long dreamed of calling our church First Interfaith Church of Lynnwood. I had served as the choir director at the First United Methodist Church in Monterey Park, California. I had sung and worked at other "First" churches. Quite frankly, I liked the sound of it. "First Interfaith." It called to me. I had even registered our new group under the name "First Interfaith Church" with the State of Washington.

But at the meeting, Heidi objected to that proposed name. She suggested that if we were sincere about being inclusive, we should know that "First" churches not only had a bit of arrogance built in (*we* were *first!*), but also the "First" churches in communities tended to be white. As I listened, I could feel my dream of "First Interfaith" fading away. Steve Crawford came up with the solution. I had created a website called Living Interfaith and had been blogging on it ever since I'd joined the Seattle Interfaith Community Church. I have believed since childhood that what counts is not the life we proclaim, but the life we live.[2] I'd been blogging about how we might *live* Interfaith. Steve suggested that we call our church Living Interfaith. And so we did.

Again, the lesson for me was to listen to what others were saying. There would be times when I would strongly advocate for my point of view. But, in this case, by listening and letting go of what was a truly minor part of the dream of Interfaith, I could tell that Heidi was right and that Steve had come up with a much better name for us—one that spoke to who we were.

What became clear to me was that I needed to embrace what can best be crystallized by a phrase from the civil rights movement: "Eyes on the Prize." The prize was a functioning, inclusive Interfaith congregation. It was not my dream of calling our church "First Interfaith."

So instead of waiting until September, the first service of the Living Interfaith Church came in March 2010. At this point there were only a few of us, maybe five people. We met at my house, and we met once a month. This time frame was born out of necessity, but it also proved to be an important schedule. I was learning how to put an Interfaith service together. With a full month between services, I had a chance to rethink, regroup, and try again.

One of the things I learned was that I was not good at improvising a sermon. My thinking is much too scattered and I have very strong opinions on too many subjects. I need the time to write the first draft of a sermon and then to weed out the extraneous opinions and pontifications that tend to distract. So after those first few months, my sermons have all been written and then read. I have never written a sermon in less than three drafts, and sometimes it takes seven or eight.

In September 2010 we officially launched the Living Interfaith Church. By then, Dilara and her husband had left for Saudi Arabia, where her husband had work. Starting with our September service, we met at the Alderwood Middle School in Lynnwood. We met in the cafeteria. Why? Because, while it looked a bit sterile, I had long since learned that every bit as important—if not more so—than any sermon I could possibly deliver was the chance for folks to meet and chat over coffee after the service.

The First Year

A group that became known as the Helping Hands continued to meet once a month. Dilara had left but Steve remained, and soon we were joined by Judy Smith, Gloria Parker, Patrick McKenna, and Bill Griffith. Others joined us as well, but for various reasons then left. Judy, Gloria, Patrick, Bill, and Steve remained. I mention this because any start-up is bound to be bumpy, and it's good to be prepared.

During this first year, there were three things I was trying to be very intentional about. The first intention was to be sure we were all on the same page. So, again, I made draft copies of my almost-finished book on Interfaith available to everyone. It was important that they understood where I was coming from and what I was trying to do. There were many things that I could be flexible about, but the essence of Interfaith as a faith was not one of them. Happily, the response to my book was positive and we moved forward as one.

The second intention was one I felt needed to be hammered home— that we would be a spiritual community built on consensus, not votes or dictum. But one problem from my own life experience was that I knew that I tend to express myself rather passionately. More than one person has viewed my passion as a "Take it or leave it" position. So I intentionally prefaced virtually everything I said at a Helping Hands meeting with, "I speak passionately, but not from on high. None of this is written in stone."

I think I was helped in this second intention by my actions. People saw that I wasn't posturing. I wasn't speaking words that were etched in stone, and I was very willing not only to listen to other points of view but also to change my mind to accommodate them. A day that made me smile was when as I was yet again saying, "None of what I'm saying is written in stone," and Patrick interrupted me with a chipper, "So stipulated. Can we move on?" This has become known as the "McKenna Stipulation," namely that everyone understands that we work by consensus, and while I have opinions, I don't think of them as any more weighty than anyone else's. From the moment the McKenna Stipulation was expressed, I knew that our commitment to consensus was real.

The third intention was to be sure that we were anchored in the community. This one I had to push a bit. A few of us became involved with cold weather shelters. But that didn't take hold as a Living Interfaith project. Some of us were interested in environmental projects, but again, nothing took hold. After several months, I pushed my particular issue: hunger. We started collecting food for the local food bank. And each year we do a bit more. Several of us have been involved in larger projects that address hunger as well.

That is how Living Interfaith was launched. As the first year progressed and we then entered our second, third, and fourth years, there were, as we like to refer to them, some joys and bumps along the road. That's for the next chapter.

The second year was spent consolidating what had happened in year 1 and continuing forward. In year 3 we finally felt comfortable enough to tackle mission and vision statements and bylaws. We needed bylaws, not only to make sure we wouldn't get sloppy with how we worked, but also because we wanted to apply for charitable status, 501(c)(3), with the IRS. It's perhaps worth noting that a church automatically has charitable status. But if we were ever to apply for a grant, we'd need official standing with the IRS. That meant a mountain of paperwork. But we did it, and received our letter of confirmation.

The Experiment

But what about our services? How often should we meet? And when? On what day? These are questions we probably should have spent a lot more time considering, but we didn't.

We decided to have our services on Sunday mornings more out of habit than anything else. We decided to meet at 11:00 a.m. because I don't wake up very quickly, and I convinced the Helping Hands that having the minister awake for the service was probably a good idea. When we met at my house, we met once a month. But when we moved from my house to the middle school, we decided on twice a month.

Why twice a month? At first this was a matter of economics. We simply couldn't afford to rent space four times a month. But as I had more time to think about it, I didn't want us to change, even though our financial situation had improved. We want to be welcoming and not exclusive. In particular, Living Interfaith is grounded in the belief that people should not have to leave their spiritual community to join ours. So the idea of having services on the second and fourth Sundays of the month was attractive, as it left all members of the congregation free on the first and third Sundays to worship elsewhere.

Several of our members have taken advantage of this. They are what I like to call bi-churched. Some, in all honesty, like the idea of only going to church twice a month and only belong to Living Interfaith.

But over time, our twice-a-month Sunday services have had both their pluses and minuses. I'm not at all convinced that we'll stay with them. We might continue meeting twice a month, but on a weeknight, or Saturday morning, or perhaps a Sunday afternoon. I would encourage anyone striving to start an Interfaith congregation to be flexible. Differing people will have differing needs. No day or time of day is holier than another.

Interfaith is a work in progress. I'll keep anyone interested updated on what we're doing by posting on our website, LivingInterfaith.org. I'd also be interested in hearing from people who start Interfaith churches (or circles) what days of the week and times they have tried, and how it's worked for them. We're in this together. Problems will come up. Changes will happen. Let's keep in touch.

Now, as promised, Dilara and Steve's thoughts on starting Living Interfaith.

The Early Days of Living Interfaith

Dilara Hafiz

I am honored to have been included as one of the founders of Living Interfaith. I met Steven frequently in 2009–2010 at both Interfaith Community Church services in Seattle and Camp Brotherhood interfaith gatherings. I was struck with his passion for Interfaith as well as his vision to begin Living Interfaith. Coming from a more structured, organized faith community of Sunni Muslims,

I was energized and liberated by the freedom to explore, which Interfaith offered to me. Although I had been heavily involved with the Arizona Interfaith Movement since 2000, I had never participated in the exciting prospect of actually beginning a new congregation of like-minded individuals from scratch.

Thus Steven, Steve, and I began meeting regularly in 2009 at Steven's house. Perhaps we all brought different visions of Living Interfaith, but those early meetings were imperative to build up trust between us. As I envision other groups following in our footsteps, beginning their own versions of Living Interfaith, I would counsel honesty and trust above all. Sitting down and sharing one's dreams can be terrifying, but the strength and confidence that came from realizing that we three had a shared vision was the reward we reaped together. From my own perspective, I was thrilled to imagine a congregation of believers and doers that could draw upon, in my opinion, the best of all the faith traditions we had encountered. As Steven emphasized in his goals for Living Interfaith, the emphasis on learning and doing was paramount. I shared his dream of a congregation that would come together in spiritual celebration and uplift, as well as actualizing the principles of Living Interfaith by reaching out to the local community and international groups.

Priorities

As I look back upon our early days, I realize that of the three of us, Steven was by far the most practical one. He took upon himself the lion's share of the legal paperwork involved with setting up the bylaws of Living Interfaith, as well as the website, the tax status, and myriad other business details. We all pitched in with the research about venues to rent for regular meetings; however, in the end, the wise decision to initially meet at Steven's house made financial sense to our fledgling congregation. Steven's generosity made Living Interfaith possible.

I admit that I enjoyed daydreaming about the ideal Interfaith service—a service that would fill in the gaps that I personally felt were present in traditional Muslim worship services. The absence of music and voices raised in song, rather than just worshipful chants, niggled at me, so of course I envisioned a musical component to our Interfaith services. I also wanted to include the observation of other faith traditions' holidays, life lessons, mantras, and rituals. I see this inclusion as an educational and spiritual expansion of one's grounding in one's own faith tradition, as well as a firm commitment to connect with others. As a Muslim, I often return to this passage from the Qur'an, which I feel speaks of the importance of interfaith knowledge:

O mankind, We have created you male and female, and appointed you races and tribes, that you may know one another. Surely the noblest among you in the sight of God is the most god-fearing of you. God is All-knowing, All-aware. (49:13)[3]

Food and Fellowship

Building a congregation from the ground up is an exciting endeavor. The glue that binds a group together requires food and fellowship as well as the shared commitment to the goals of the organization. As we planned for the first service of Living Interfaith, we all agreed upon the importance of time for us to get to know each other, ideally in conversation after the service. Thus the potluck element of Living Interfaith was born. As memory serves, we initially had some evening meetings where we reached out to like-minded individuals who had expressed interest in Living Interfaith. These early dinners served as a gentle introduction to the idea of the Living Interfaith congregation, time to share dreams and find common ground. I think that these early meetings cemented the foundation of Living Interfaith so that the first services included friends all happy to embark on this voyage together.

I'm thrilled that the seeds of Living Interfaith have sprouted so successfully, although I am no longer an active member, due to distance. The very fact that Living Interfaith continues to grow and move from strength to strength confirms my belief that interfaith experiences enrich all those who are fortunate to participate in them. No matter where I am, I will always seek out a group of like-minded individuals to nourish my spirituality.

Living Interfaith's Origin

Steve Crawford

I met Steven Greenebaum at the Interfaith Community Sanctuary in Seattle, Washington. It was and continues to be a community-based organization where members of all faiths are welcome and works to promote peace and understanding among its members and visitors. It does not promote Interfaith as a religious faith. It functions as a way for people of different faiths to interact, worship, and support each other.

Steven's announcement that he was leaving to start another Interfaith church was intriguing to me and I approached him with my interest. He invited me to participate in its birth and I began my involvement. I remained a member of the Interfaith Community Sanctuary throughout the creation of the Living Interfaith Church and am an active member of both organizations today.

We began as a small group, meeting at Steven's house. Initially, we met to get to know each other and share our religious and spiritual experiences. We did this not to convince each other of anything but to simply start the process in an open and non-judgmental manner. It is important to note that none of us had any experience in creating a church or a new religious faith. In the weeks that followed, our group lost members for a variety of reasons; none of them had anything to do with religious arguments. We eventually coalesced into the founding group of three people—Dilara, Steven, and me. It is from this humble beginning that our church began.

We started our services at Steven's home as our numbers and finances were very modest. We grew slowly until we had about ten solid members, at which point we rented space at a middle school that continues to be our home today. Our journey was a step-by-small-step process founded on the strength of our ideas and fellowship with each other. We didn't know how our church would manifest but had faith that it would.

I am contributing this section to speak to people who would like to attend a Living Interfaith Church but are unable to do so. If you would like to worship in a Living Interfaith Church where you live, you will have to start your own. It may seem to be a daunting task to start a church, but you are not alone. The basic structure of Interfaith as a religious faith has already been presented in Steven's first book, *The Interfaith Alternative*. "Our Covenant and Six Fundamental Assumptions" appear in this book (page 138) and on the church's website.

The power of these ideas will be your ally. They will attract people who are interested in community worship and fellowship without the baggage of trying to prove that one religious faith is superior to others. If you have questions about how services are structured, you can certainly contact us through our website, LivingInterfaith.org. It is important to note that we do not expect new Living Interfaith churches to be carbon copies of ours. Everything is flavored and colored by the people directly involved. I'm sure this will be the case as you create your own church.

History is replete with conflicts rooted in religious faith in which one faith doggedly asserts its supremacy above all others. These conflicts have resulted in human misery, ranging from mild annoyance to outright physical violence. Living Interfaith offers a viable way out of this persistent quicksand that has plagued humanity for so long. If you are called by these ideas, start your own church and help spread the bloom of religious peace.

14

JOYS AND BUMPS ALONG THE WAY

Never having started a church before, I have no idea how typical or atypical our experience was. But I doubt it will come as a shock to anyone that, as with any new enterprise, some things worked and some things didn't. We called them "joys and bumps" and made discussion of this a regular part of the agenda at our Helping Hands meeting. Choosing the word "bumps" has intent behind it. "I encountered a bump" feels far less confrontational than "I have a concern" or "This bothers me." Bumps in the road are a part of life. We all experience them along the way. If we learn from them, acknowledging our bumps can be a positive way to smooth out the road into the future.

Having designated time to acknowledge our bumps allows us to address what might otherwise fester into a major problem before it does. It also helps to reinforce that bumps are to be expected, and not to be feared. Our hope is to bring them up, address them, and move on. Here, simply as examples, are a few of the joys and bumps we've experienced thus far along the way.

Joys
The People
One of the most significant joys for me has been the people that Interfaith generally attracts. People drawn to Interfaith tend to be open-minded and indeed quite curious about other points of view. It's difficult, though not

impossible, to be dogmatic and embrace Interfaith as a faith. So discussions, while lively, are rarely lines-in-the-sand sorts of affairs. This, as I think about it, is probably what made the second joy possible.

Working by Consensus

Let's be honest here. It's one thing to want to have a group that makes decisions by consensus. It's quite another to actually do it. But, remarkably, our board (the Helping Hands) has, to date, never needed to take a vote on a major decision. Thus far, we have always been able to come to a consensus. When an issue comes up, we talk about it. We always try to get to the "why" behind a matter of possible contention. In the end, we just keep talking and listening to each other until we come to mutual agreement.

I believe an essential part of our approach to consensus succeeding is that all of us have embraced the idea that the inclusive "we" has to win. It's not a question of "I win and you lose." Nor is it "I lose and you win." Neither of those two outcomes is satisfactory or satisfying. The question for discussion is always, "How do we arrive at a solution where *we* win this?" It sounds so simple, but unfortunately this is not how our culture teaches us to relate. In a sense, it goes back to our cultural buy-in to the idea of a zero-sum world, where every loss is balanced by somebody's win, and every win is balanced by somebody's loss. Consensus rejects the zero-sum paradigm. Consensus means that if you lose, I can't win. And if I lose, you can't win. Consensus teaches that the only way forward is to fully embrace "us." The only win that has meaning is if we *all* win. It is very Interfaith and very dear to my heart, though I'll admit that it can also be a tad unwieldy at times.

This was particularly in evidence as we adopted "Our Covenant and Six Fundamental Assumptions" as well as our bylaws. Wording here was important. There were a few times when it took at least three meetings—that's three months—to resolve an issue. But we were always able to come to a compromise that all of us could not simply live with but embrace. This has been a source of great pleasure and satisfaction to me.[1]

Learning about Diverse Paths

A third joy is how much I've learned. I entered into ministry with a solid grasp of Judaism and Protestant Christianity, with a decent grasp of Catholicism as well, and a smattering of Buddhism and Paganism. But in establishing Living Interfaith Church I have learned so much more. As but one example, I had never really known much at all about the Baha'i faith. That is changing, and as I learn more about this path and others, I feel my spirit grow as well as smile.

It has been no great surprise, but still a great joy, to realize that none of us is a threat to the other. Each of us reflects the sacred in a different way. It's like living in a wonderful sacred house filled with many, many rooms. I have my own room. It is mine, decorated and organized in ways that are familiar and comfortable to me. No one else's room is a threat to mine. But it is broadening, not to mention fascinating, to visit other people's rooms. And, extending the metaphor even further, it is truly grand to get together for meals and discussions and talk about why I find a certain kind of bed so restful, and discover that a friend never feels relaxed on that kind of bed and loves to sprawl on one much softer or firmer.

Bumps

I don't mean to shortchange the joys of an Interfaith church. But I have the feeling that our bumps may be more instructive. So here let's get into a bit more detail.

The Bump That Wasn't

It is definitely humbling and possibly instructive that the one bump I was truly anxious about and had with some trepidation tried to prepare for never happened. I was concerned about, if not fixated on, the person who might be drawn to an Interfaith service in order to proselytize and set people straight about the true faith, whatever that person might view the true faith to be. I had imagined and then reimagined what I might need to say or do to keep things from getting out of hand.

But this was the great advantage of beginning with a small core group of people and bringing them along with me. The few times true believers have shown up, and they have, I haven't needed to say a word. Our congregation has a welcome mat out for people of all spiritual paths. But proselytizing true believers quickly feel out of step. The congregation was very polite, more bemused than offended, but also uninterested in engaging.

A Small Bump

Interfaith, as a faith, is still very new to people. Folks are so used to inter-faith events that they assume that Interfaith is the same thing. Some who haven't really warmed to interfaith exchanges tend to stay away. Other people who find that interfaith (with a lowercase "i") fits right into their comfort zone become rather uncomfortable when they discover we prac-tice Interfaith (with a capital "I"). There haven't as yet been any overblown incidents, but the bump is there.

Two items need to be stressed. The first is that most of us are much too used to the either/or mode of evaluating spiritual paths. So when people find that we are Interfaith and not interfaith, the assumption is that we think we are superior, better, or at the very least that we don't value inter-faith. But as a faith, Interfaith teaches us that this is not a matter of one is right and the other wrong. They are different but the truth of it is that when practiced by loving, compassionate people, both interfaith and Inter-faith are equally profound.

The second item is a short statement of how Interfaith is different from interfaith—not better, but different. When "interfaith" is used, it is as an adjective, describing a mode of engagement. An interfaith dialogue is a dia-logue between people of differing faiths. An interfaith project is a project in which people of differing faiths participate. An interfaith service is a service that includes snippets from differing faiths.

What makes Interfaith different is that it is a noun and describes a faith—not a mode of engagement, but a faith. Interfaith, as a faith, takes as an article of faith that all our spiritual paths are equally valid if practiced with love and compassion. Interfaith, as a faith, does not deny the many differences between our spiritual paths, and acknowledges that those dif-ferences are both cultural and doctrinal. What Interfaith, as a faith, says is that while our spiritual paths are different, the goal at the mountaintop remains the same: to act with love and compassion, in community with others.

A Somewhat Larger Bump

This bump was wholly of my own doing. As Living Interfaith got going, there was a lot of work to be done. Starting a new faith and a new church is hard and time-consuming work. I put my life into it, day after day. But others, while they may become very interested in Interfaith, have their own lives and their own work. I got so involved with my work that I forgot that.

The bump came when others, seeing how much time I was putting in, in their compassion and with their good hearts, volunteered to shoulder some of the load. I welcomed this, both because a social life is a very nice thing to have now and then, and also because I was determined to make sure this was a group effort, rather than a personal one. So, particularly in the first few years, I tended to off-load rather large chunks of work to people who volunteered for it.

The result was that several fine people who had joined us and wanted to help burned out. Having volunteered to do too much of the work, given the many other demands on their time, they were then faced with being unable to finish what they had volunteered to do. They took it as their failings and several simply disappeared. But it wasn't their failing; it was mine. I have learned to be much more careful in off-loading work. I still want a life. But I don't want it at the expense of others.

The Huge Bump

What I would call the "Numbers Trap" has come close to derailing us, not once but several times. "Why aren't we larger?" It's a reasonable question and deserves a reasonable answer. But beneath that reasonable question lies something that is truly unreasonable. The unreasonable part is the buy-in to the supersize-it mentality that we are subjected to every day of every year. Bigger is better. Bigger is always better. The great goal is to be *big*.

In a sense, this is part of the "keeping up with the neighbors" mentality that has driven American consumerism. It's not healthy and it's not helpful. I would strongly urge a return to quality over quantity. Just as cheap can be very expensive, so can quantity. If, as a church, our driving purpose is our numbers, then we may lose track of what had been our original purpose—safe, sacred space for Interfaith as a faith.

Yet the call of numbers can be seductive. Our church began very small— maybe five of us. Then, within a year, we doubled to ten. Then we averaged fifteen at a service. As a minister, it was more than nice; it was gratifying to see all those faces, representing not only individual human beings who had made the choice to participate in Interfaith but also a rich diversity of spiritual paths. But from time to time, weather and other circumstances intervened, and I can recall vividly how it felt the very first time I had a congregation of three seated in front of me. Three! My heart sank. The first question I asked myself was, What had I done? What mistake had I made? A further and much darker question hounded me on my way home and for the next several days: Had I killed Interfaith by my shortcomings?

But slogging my way through these doubts has turned out to be hugely helpful. I would work on a sermon for a day, sometimes two or three days. And then, sometimes, I would present it to four people. I understand now that numbers truly don't matter. Those four people deserved and got my best. *That* is what's important. What remains crucial is creating safe, sacred space, and we've done that, whether there are four people there or more often ten to fifteen, and from time to time twenty-five to thirty. By the end of our third year I stopped paying attention to numbers, let alone being concerned or pleased. At this point, I don't feel vindication when there are a lot of people and I don't feel threatened when there are only a few. It is freeing to understand and embrace that it's not about me or the numbers.

That was my journey. I mentioned above that numbers came close to derailing us several times because I wasn't the only one of us nearly seduced by the call of numbers. This was something many of us had to work through. If you start an Interfaith group, you may—indeed, probably will—face it yourself. When you do, remember that you are not alone. Hang in there.

Interfaith as a faith is a paradigm shift. Interfaith involves embracing the sacred in a way that we simply haven't done before. Even for people who feel a strong attraction and resonance with Interfaith, the old paradigm of right belief may be so strongly embedded within that it's hard, if not impossible, for them to embrace the new paradigm. As mentioned before, it will take time. It may well take a generation or two—or more. During that time, what is essential is that there are small Interfaith groups—as many as we can muster—to create safe, sacred space and show that we can indeed celebrate and nurture each other in our diversity.

If we grow, terrific! Hey, I'm all for growing. It certainly helps with the financial side of things when there are more people to help with the ongoing costs. And let's admit it: There is a certain joy to numbers. But that said, what remains essential is to have Interfaith communities, of whatever size, as examples of moving past right belief into mutual respect and celebration. We can embrace each other, we can learn from each other, we can respect our diverse spiritual paths, all without losing our own spiritual selves. I can remain Jewish, and still celebrate Christmas with you out of respect for you and how you engage the sacred. I can remain Muslim, and still celebrate the Buddha with you out of respect for you and how you engage the sacred.

I believe strongly and passionately, not only that we can celebrate our own spiritual paths as well as the paths of others but also that by doing so we will grow closer to the sacred. Right now, there are only a small number of us who both believe this and are also willing to put these beliefs into practice. But the positive reaction of people all over the country—indeed, all over the world—to *The Interfaith Alternative* helps me to understand that we can do this. We can create a more loving, compassionate world. And it's worth doing.

Numbers right now just aren't that important. What is important is that Interfaith communities exist and are nurtured. As people begin to awaken to the new paradigm of Interfaith, there need to be communities they can join. This is what counts. Numbers are pleasant. Safe, sacred space is what is crucial.

A Bit Deeper

Questions for Discussion

Has a need for numbers ever gotten in the way of your doing something that called to you? If so, how did you feel about that? Why do you think we get so caught up in size (the size of a car, a house, a social club, a congregation)?

How would you explain to someone the difference between an interfaith congregation and an Interfaith congregation? Could you do it without making a judgment between them?

While I encourage people to discuss their spiritual paths, I also encourage them to avoid arguments. What would be the difference between discussing your path with someone who walks a different path, and arguing about it?

15

SOME THOUGHTS ON INTERFAITH MINISTRY

Given the continued confusion between interfaith and Interfaith, it may be helpful to review the differences with a focus on ministry, always with the oft-repeated caution that "different" does not mean "better" or "worse." As example, carrots and oranges, while the same color, are assuredly not the same food. If our goal is to get vitamin C, we might well extol the virtues of oranges. This doesn't make oranges a better food than carrots. Carrots are definitely a better source of vitamin A. But if we specifically want vitamin C, we'll head toward the orange bin.

That said, Interfaith ministry, as opposed to interfaith ministry, has its own bin for a couple of important reasons. A cornerstone to Interfaith ministry is an abiding faith that there is no hierarchy to humanity's diverse ways of approaching the sacred. Believing in God is not better or worse than not believing. Christianity is not inherently better or worse than Islam. Perhaps even more importantly, Interfaith offers mutual respect for our diverse spiritual paths and mutual celebration.

An Interfaith minister then needs to feel comfortable not only with Christians but with the celebration of Christian holy days, with Muslims and the celebration of Muslim holy days, with Humanists and the celebration of important Humanist days, and so on. In Interfaith, all these spiritual paths are recognized, respected, and celebrated without any attempt at hierarchy.

Some folks will come to Interfaith cleaving to a particular spiritual path. This is not a contradiction. An Interfaith minister will seek to help these people along the path they have chosen. Some, on the other hand, may come to Interfaith without any specific path that calls to them, but rather a feeling of being called by compassion, love, and community. For these people, an Interfaith minister's calling is not to help each of them find the right path but rather to guide them in their all-important quest to be better human beings.

Regardless of spiritual path, the paramount question in Interfaith ministry remains, "How can I help you to be a better human being?" With that question at heart, and keeping the person's preferred spiritual path in mind, the Interfaith minister is called to assist, guide, and occasionally even prod, but never to instruct.

Thus an Interfaith minister is called to be a keeper of the open mind, rather than a Keeper of the Faith. Possibly the most important gift an Interfaith minister can bring to others is leadership by example in creating safe, sacred space. As we get more used to it, this particular gift may become more common, but at the moment—like it or not—we still live in a right-belief world. Safe, sacred space for sharing our diverse spiritual paths remains crucial.

At present, in our rather binary world, there are two differing approaches to spirituality that have squared off. One approach says that all our spiritual paths are the same and that we should ignore our differences. The other approach says that all our spiritual paths are different, incompatible, and irreconcilable—we can forge truces, alliances, or even talk to one another, but we cannot truly come together.

What makes life for an Interfaith minister challenging is that Interfaith gravitates toward neither approach. Interfaith, as a faith, teaches that our differing traditions are to be respected and honored, and most definitely not ignored. Yet Interfaith also teaches that, as members of the human family, we must not allow those differences to divide us.

It's time to return to the example of Mount Fuji, and the Japanese folk saying reminding us that there are many paths to the top. We have, if you will, been standing for millennia at the bottom of a great mountain. At the top of that mountain is our mutual goal of love, compassion, and community. There are any number of worthwhile, yet differing paths—some quite different from others—that lead to the top of that mountain. But rather than choose a path and walk it, we've been standing at the foot of the mountain, throwing rocks at each other over whose path to the mountaintop is best.

The goal of Interfaith is to help us get to the mountaintop and to stop throwing rocks. Part of the purpose of Interfaith ministry then is to be a trail guide. The job of the Interfaith minister is not to tell people which path is right, but to help them along the path of their choosing, or to explore the differing paths until a path that suits their particular spiritual needs can be found.

This is a crucial aspect of Interfaith ministry. An Interfaith minister is not a judge, but rather a spiritual facilitator. This notion harkens back to the essence of ministry: service. "How can I help you along your path to love, compassion, and community?" This is the primary question an Interfaith minister asks.

We should discuss one other crucial aspect of Interfaith ministry. I believe that Interfaith's lack of doctrine and dogma gives an Interfaith minister both the opportunity and the responsibility to lead by example, rather than by proclamation. It is at least my hope that the long list of guilt-inducing "shoulds" that can sometimes accompany a spiritual path may be replaced by more actively positive "dos."

As example, the minister is not preaching that we should respect other ways of approaching the sacred; the minister leads by respecting differing approaches to the sacred in his or her own life. The minister is not preaching that we should help those who are in need, but leads by being an active part in the community helping the hungry, the homeless, or the disabled. Just as important, the minister is not preaching that we should admit it when we screw up and apologize, but leads by acknowledging her or his mistakes and then asking for forgiveness.

Thus the essence of Interfaith leadership and ministry is being open and authentic, a sort of "What you see is what you get" approach to matters spiritual. I believe this can be a tremendously positive thing, both for the minister and for the congregation. It might even be positive for the world at large.

Voices of Interfaith

Steve Crawford

I started my journey to Interfaith through a simple and non-denominational Christianity taught to me by my mother. I left Christianity in my late teens and began the process of exploring various religious practices and philosophies throughout my sixty years of life.

My spiritual tradition is Life itself. The gift of consciousness is an extraordinary opportunity to experience, think, and contribute to our world. My goals are to live in peace and bring loving acceptance with my presence.

I chose Interfaith as a religious faith because it frees people from doctrinal control and instead focuses on living in peace and goodwill, while promoting social justice. It embraces any ideology that results in loving action. It is a valuable addition to the religious world that has been rife with conflict. It also works as an agent of peace between the religious and secular worlds.

Part IV

RESOURCES FOR AN INTERFAITH COMMUNITY

To stand an old bromide on its head, not only do we sometimes miss the forest for the trees, but much too often we also seem to be missing the trees for the forest. I suppose no one will be shocked that the Interfaith approach is to respect both the trees and the forest. But what does that mean?

The forest, if you will, is formed by the basic tenet of Interfaith as a faith. There is no hierarchy to our spiritual paths. We affirm that all of our paths call us to lives of love, compassion, and community. At the same time, those paths are exceedingly diverse in describing how we are to get there. Interfaith, as a faith, does not call on us to ignore these differences. Rather, we are called not only to respect but also to honor our diverse answers to the call of the sacred. More than that, we are called on to cease dividing ourselves, to recognize our common humanity, and to work together— even as we honor our differences—toward our common goal of love, compassion, and community.

But that lovely Interfaith forest remains merely a dream until and unless some real and specific trees are planted and then nurtured. A forest may begin with a single tree, or small stand of trees, but it begins with actual trees—not simply hopes or dreams. It's the difference between Johnny Appleseed preaching trees and planting them.

Moreover, as any person interested in forestry will share, a healthy forest needs a diversity of trees. So as we begin to look at some of the specifics of Living Interfaith's contribution to this newly planted forest called Interfaith, I think it is helpful to view it as planting some important trees but not the whole forest. In discussing what Living Interfaith has attempted, I'm by no means saying this is or should be the only way to engage in Interfaith. I would hope for and encourage the cultivation of a wonderfully diverse forest. But I do believe, and certainly hope, that by sharing what we've been doing at Living Interfaith, and why, our experiences can be useful both to those who would follow in our footsteps as well as those who may say, "We are interested in Interfaith, but we want to pursue a different approach."

With this in mind, in this section on resources for an Interfaith community, the essence of practical Interfaith, we'll first take a deeper look at Interfaith ministry and then explore three ways that Living Interfaith has attempted to nurture the beginnings of a healthy, Interfaith forest. What follows will provide more detail. Here is an outline to set the stage for that detail.

Ministry

We'll look at two differing aspects of ministry. The first answers the question: What should we look for in an Interfaith minister? The question might be asked as a group begins to meet, or perhaps after it has been meeting for a while and makes a decision that an Interfaith minister is needed to give the group a more spiritually nurturing experience.

The second is a start at answering the question: "I think I want to be an Interfaith minister. What would that mean? How would that look?" As always, these chapters are intended as a beginning point, not the final word on the subject.

The Interfaith Service

Is a service the only way to embrace Interfaith? Certainly not. Then why have a service? That's a reasonable question to ask. I believe our spiritual paths and our spiritual natures call to our hearts as well as our minds. If Interfaith dwells only in our mind, I believe it becomes more of an intellectual exercise and less a spiritual one. Sadly, many high-minded philosophies and love-centered spiritual paths throughout human history have been accompanied by anything but high-minded and love-centered actions. For me, if Interfaith is to succeed as a spiritual path, it must unite heart and mind in common purpose.

So what does this have to do with having a service? A service, filled with song, inclusive ritual and prayer, as well as messages that speak to our Interfaith sensibilities, can nourish our whole being—our mind as well as our heart. It can also help to build community among us, all of us, even as we honor and acknowledge our diversity.

More than that, if we include and experience in these services the differing ways our spiritual paths approach the sacred, both our hearts and our minds are broadened. I'm reminded of the U.S. senator who was adamantly against gay marriage until he realized that his own son was gay and wanted to marry the person whom he loved and to whom he was committed. Suddenly the senator understood, opened his heart, and changed his position. There is truth and much profundity in the saying "To truly know another, walk a mile in his moccasins." Services that celebrate and allow us to share our diverse spiritual paths help us to walk in one another's moccasins.

For me, another crucial aspect of our services comes at those times when we honor a specific spiritual path's holy day—Passover in Judaism, as example, or Epiphany in Christianity. One thing we have been intentional about at Living Interfaith is to share our beliefs and our paths, not explain them. This means that while I have led services that honor Jewish holy days, I have never led one that honors a Christian, Baha'i, Buddhist, Muslim, or other spiritual path's holy day. I never want to be in the position of speaking about what "they" believe. When we celebrate a Baha'i holy day, a member of the Baha'i faith speaks. When we honor a Muslim holy day, a member of the Muslim faith speaks. It is always, always in the context of sharing. We share ourselves as we share our spiritual paths.

Surely a service is not the only way to accomplish this. But it is a good and powerful way, and it is how we have chosen to practice an important aspect of our Interfaith. In that context, a few chapters on, we'll discuss the specifics of how we put a service together.

I can't leave the idea of a service without mentioning the strong need to complete every service with food and conversation. At present Living Interfaith meets at a middle school. We meet in the cafeteria. It takes a good half hour every Sunday to transform that cafeteria into sacred space. But it's worth the time because meeting in the cafeteria allows us to complete each service with coffee, a shared potluck of goodies, and conversation. Time to eat together and talk together is important. It's for that reason that I don't say, "After the service we have coffee and conversation," but rather that we "complete the service" with it. I deeply believe that creating time to be together and build community needs to be considered part of every service. It goes back to our desire to connect mind and heart.

Liturgy

After the chapter titled "Anatomy of an Interfaith Service" comes a chapter of Interfaith liturgy. "Liturgy," as used here, involves simply the written or spoken Interfaith parts of a service, or rituals that are used to help make our service Interfaith. We had to start from scratch. Once again, the purpose of sharing our liturgy is not to establish the one right way, but to help new Interfaith groups as they begin so that they don't feel a need to reinvent the wheel. As we add liturgy, we'll add it to the LivingInterfaith. org website.

Some texts bear repeating. I believe it is especially helpful to have a common statement that, while short, can serve both to remind longtimers why they are there and to help a newcomer understand what Interfaith is about. That is the purpose of beginning every service with "Our Joint Affirmation."

For us it is also important to have responsive readings, where a reader makes the first statement and the entire congregation responds. This helps to emphasize that a service is a group experience, that we're in this together. For that reason, at Living Interfaith the person who leads the reading changes from Sunday to Sunday. Only rarely is the minister the reader. Again, in the search for Interfaith responsive readings, we have frequently found it necessary to write our own. But it should be noted that roughly half of our services are on Interfaith themes, and the other half celebrate and honor a particular spiritual path. Whenever possible, on a day that celebrates, say, Buddhism, the responsive reading is from the Buddhist tradition.

In terms of prayers, which may be said aloud in front of the congregation, or perhaps spoken by everyone, there are many prayers already out there that support an Interfaith sensibility.[1] But from time to time, a specific need has prompted us to create our own prayers, and those are printed here.

Lastly, as the Interfaith forest begins to grow and thrive, specific liturgies will be needed. I had the honor of creating an Interfaith "Child Dedication." We also have created a brief ceremony welcoming new members to the congregation. That is included as well. The crucial aspect of these and any other Interfaith rituals is to be inclusive. Particularly with the Child Dedication, we keep in mind that there may be family members who cleave to a particular spiritual path.

Structure: Some Possibly Helpful Documents

I have also supplied an appendix at the end of the book that has to do with official documents. These are offered so that new Interfaith communities do not have to start from the beginning. But a caution may be in order. We didn't write our mission statement, our vision statement, or our bylaws until our third year. The only document we began with was our "Our Covenant and Six Assumptions." I think this was helpful. Why?

A new church or congregation needs some coherent statement to rally around, to articulate the essence of why they are coming together. For us, this was Our Covenant and Six Assumptions. But that said, it takes time for people to get a feel for who they are, and to learn to trust one another. For me, mission and vision statements should wait until people have been gathering together for a while, long enough to begin to gain a sense of who they are as a community. That happened for us in our third year, but there's nothing magical about that number. Maybe it will take you only two years, then again maybe four. But the important thing is to let it take time ... and meanwhile, start meeting. Start getting to know each other.

After a multiyear, see-what-shakes-out period—when those who joined at first but aren't that interested leave, and those who didn't know about you at first but love what you are about have joined—it's time to think about mission and vision statements. In these statements, everyone who is interested has had a chance to share her or his mind and heart and opinion.

As for bylaws, having adopted ours in our third year, I now feel that was a bit too soon. We needed bylaws in order to apply to the IRS for 501(c)(3) status, and we needed that status because we were about to embark on a fund-raising campaign to create an Interfaith curriculum for the education of our children. I think it would have been better to wait until year 5, but that's just my opinion.

If everyone is genuinely committed to consensus, then bylaws are much less important as you begin—you'll still want them eventually, but not immediately. On the other hand, if making decisions by consensus proves difficult, bylaws can be a lifesaver. Bylaws, among other things, act as a brake against arbitrary actions on the part of the minister, the board, or whomever.

16

CHOOSING AN INTERFAITH MINISTER

L et's say that you and some others have been meeting and discussing Interfaith. You've decided to form an Interfaith congregation, and that may mean finding a minister. What are some things to look for? What are some things to look out for?

In over forty years of working in churches, synagogues, and temples it has been my intense and happy privilege to know several nurturing, spirit-filled ministers.[1] It has also been my equally intense and supremely educational adventure to have known several toxic ministers. I am but one person, and have clearly been exposed to a limited sampling. Nonetheless, I think it may be helpful for me to share some of the lessons I have gleaned from these experiences.

The first lesson I'd like to share is that toxic ministers come in a variety of flavors. Nurturing, spirit-filled ministers all seem to share some very specific traits, regardless of the spiritual path they follow.

The Blessing of the Spirit-Filled Minister

Let's start with the positive. What are the shared qualities of the spirit-filled minister? Spirit-filled ministers know themselves. This does not mean they've stopped growing or changing. Rather, having discovered who they are, they can embrace that growth and those changes without fear of losing their way. They are comfortable in their own shoes. They have plenty to do and little to prove. At the same time, they are also deeply humble. Knowing who they are, they know, as well, who they are not. Being comfortable with who they are, they are also well aware that they are human.

These spirit-filled ministers lead by example far more than by any list of "shoulds" or "should nots" proclaimed from the pulpit. This assuredly does not mean that even the best of ministers won't stumble from time to time as they lead. But what is empowering and inspiring is that with nothing to prove they are able to admit to stumbling, and in that way are able to model humanity—not perfection, humanity. I believe an important part of leading is modeling how to deal with making mistakes and, from time to time, how to deal with falling flat on one's face.

My life has been immeasurably enriched by these amazing and wonderful people. To have been fortunate enough to have been in their presence and to be able to call some of them friend has both inspired and guided me. These are ministers to emulate, and I have tried—imperfectly, to be sure, but I have tried.

But, of course, not every minister is spirit-filled. Which brings us to toxic ministry.

The Curse of the Toxic Minister

The interesting thing, at least to me, is that most toxic ministers aren't obviously toxic. If they were, they probably wouldn't be ministers, or at least they wouldn't be hired by any congregation in the first place. While some toxic ministers may completely decimate the congregation they are with, most demoralize and materially weaken their congregations. I've witnessed the latter in action. Three examples of toxic ministers follow. I share them because they exemplify three very different forms of toxic ministry.

One toxic minister was also one of the nicest people I've known. As long as I knew him he was friendly, and wanted to help. This is important to understand. He was, and I believe still is, a good person. He wanted to do the right thing. But deep inside, I came to learn, he believed himself unworthy, unlikable, and a fraud. I think his overriding fear was that the world, and, more importantly, his congregation, would at some point discover that he's really not a good person or a good minister. Because of this relentless fear, his primary motivation in ministry was neither leading nor helping, but being liked. When his actions lacked ethics, it was not out of malevolence, but fear. He needed to be reassured over and over again that he was both respected and the leader.

Another toxic minister was completely different. He was one of the most supremely self-confident people I've ever meet. He firmly saw himself as the strong right hand of God, and he was there to let you know it. He seemed to take it as self-evident that the world revolved around him. I'd had my fill and left before it happened, but it was not surprising when I learned he'd had an affair with a married woman he was counseling.

My last example of a toxic minister is the minister who sees ministry as a career, and who wants to climb the professional ladder. I've known a couple such ministers. Again, these weren't bad people. Indeed, one was a friend. But both of them saw their current congregations more as a part of their resumes than communities to serve. For both of them, having an eye on the future made it hard to focus on the present. Not that their intentions were bad. But focusing on "How will this look?" turned the congregations into stepping-stones. It made it much harder to commit to "How can I help?"

Frankly, I think viewing ministry as a profession can be as toxic to the minister as politics is to the person who wins elective office seeking to be a professional public servant. Ministers whose home, health care, and children's education depend both on a salary and having their contract renewed, may find their values skewed with, shall we say, unfortunate results.

I'm sure there are an infinite number of other ways a minister may be toxic. I cite these examples simply because I have seen them in action.

Finding a Spirit-Filled Minister

A spirit-filled minister doesn't come from any specific background. I have a particular bias in favor of older ministers, as many of us need a good portion of our lives behind us before we really know who we are and can accumulate enough experience to appreciate the diversity of humanity. I include myself in this group, as I became a minister at age sixty. But one of the toxic ministers mentioned above became a minister late in his life, and I'm currently working with a twenty-nine-year-old woman whom I believe will become a superb minister. So, again, we need to look at the individual, not the age, gender, or whatever.

That said, an important source for Interfaith ministers might well be retired ministers—rabbis, imams, monks—who have lived their faith but come to the conclusion that there is no one right path and are looking for a broader spiritual path than the one they've walked. I would love to see at least some of our future Interfaith ministers called Brother Rabbi Joe Smith, or Sister Reverend Julia Brown.[2]

Why reference their path? First, to respect it. Second, I strongly believe in truth in packaging. Every member of the Living Interfaith Church knows both that I'm Jewish and that it doesn't matter to me that the overwhelming majority of them are not. I think it's helpful to lay one's spiritual path out there. That's why I tend to say that my faith is Interfaith, and my spiritual path is Judaism.

So, regardless of age, gender, or background, what are we looking for? Here are a few questions you might want to ask of anyone seeking to be an Interfaith minister:

1. Do you see a difference between humility and lack of self-confidence? How would you describe that difference?

2. What is your spiritual path? Why do you walk it? Why do you think other people don't?

3. If you believe in God, why do you think other people don't? If you don't believe in God, why do you think other people do?

4. If you believe in abortion rights, how would you counsel someone with a tough abortion decision who believes abortion is wrong? If you believe abortion is wrong, how would you counsel someone with a tough abortion decision who believes in abortion rights?

The point of these questions—and any others you may come up with—is to try to understand how a potential minister thinks and applies his or her beliefs. At the root of these questions is my strong belief that the job of a minister is not to know the answer, as if there were "the answer," but to be a spiritual companion to others so they may find answers that help them. Or, to put it more succinctly: An Interfaith minister does not dispense truth; an Interfaith minister dispenses guidance. In your questions, one of your primary tasks is to discern if your prospective minister is a dispenser of truth or of guidance.

To Ordain or Not Ordain: That's a Good Question

Most organized spiritual paths have gatekeepers, who at one point or another will make a judgment as to whether a person should be ordained or recognized by that faith as a spiritual leader. From the contact I've had, either firsthand with such folks or secondhand by listening to friends who have gone through the ordination process, I think many of those gatekeepers are frankly looking the wrong way. But that comes from what may be a fundamental parting of the ways over what the primary duty of a spiritual leader is.

As will come as no particular surprise, I don't see the primary duty of a spiritual leader as being the keeper of the faith. Yes, it is good to know the history of our own spiritual path, whatever that path may be. There is much truth in the expression "To know where we are going, we must know from whence we have come." And, yes, it is good to know the basic tenets of our own spiritual path. But isn't the primary duty of a spiritual leader to give guidance and to be of comfort in times of hardship and grief, not lay down immutable rules?

That said, should Interfaith ministers be ordained and, if so, how? I would strongly caution against simply accepting people who have a piece of paper stating that they have been ordained. The question is always, Ordained by whom? What were the standards? What did the person learn? And more important than any other criteria, What sort of person is it who seeks to minister?

Simply because I think it would be helpful, I do hope that there will develop over time an education for Interfaith ministry. But for now at least, I would encourage Interfaith congregations to establish a two-year internship for an Interfaith minister, ordained elsewhere or not. Then, if it seems to be a good fit, the congregation ordains and accepts that person as minister while at the same time, in the same ceremony, the person ordained and accepted as minister accepts and commits to the congregation.

17

I Think I Want to Be an Interfaith Minister

Ministry is a calling. It can be an important, beautiful, spiritually rewarding calling, but I think it is a mistake to look to ministry as a profession. Not that long ago, in our church newsletter, I cautioned those who might consider Interfaith ministry.

> My advice to people who feel called to Interfaith ministry is, "Don't quit your day job." Be a hospital chaplain and an Interfaith minister. Or be a baker and an Interfaith minister. Or be a carpenter and be an Interfaith minister. This has the double advantage of keeping a minister grounded in the real world, and also helping a new Interfaith congregation keep its expenses down.

I could be wrong—it's happened many, many times before—but while I do think Interfaith will grow, I believe it will grow slowly.[1] Recall the section on starting an Interfaith church (page 72) and the importance of creating safe, sacred space, not numbers (page 65). Thus, if only from a purely economic standpoint, a person who hopes to make a living as an Interfaith minister should probably do some serious rethinking.

That said, some of us will feel ourselves called to the important work of Interfaith ministry even as we realize that it won't pay the rent or put food on the table. What then? What do we need to know? I can't and don't pretend to have a comprehensive answer. But I would like to share some of what has been helpful to me.

Some Possibly Helpful Thoughts on Preparing for Interfaith Ministry

A quick cautionary note: What is offered below may apply to all ministry. Then again, it may not. It is offered specifically with reference to the needs of Interfaith ministry.

Know and Be Comfortable with Yourself

This may seem self-evident. But in point of fact it isn't. When I studied at Seattle University's School of Theology and Ministry, I was profoundly taken aback at the number of people I found there who seemed to be studying ministry to find themselves. Not that finding oneself is unimportant. It's huge. The quest to find oneself is a beautiful and valuable journey. But I believe that we need to be well on our way toward finding ourself before we embark upon Interfaith ministry. Why? Perhaps first and foremost, I believe Interfaith ministers need to be so secure in their own self and path that they can help others on a completely different path without in any way feeling threatened.

Why is this so important? If I'm concerned about finding my own path, my guard will be up when I'm dealing with yours. It's hard, if not impossible, to be accepting of another's path, let alone be respectful and helpful, if I'm still struggling to find my own. If I'm measuring my path against yours, then that measurement will be where my true energy dwells—whether I wish it or not. Only when measuring paths is no longer important, when I am securely and comfortably walking my own path while recognizing that there are other wonderful paths as well, can I truly direct my efforts where they belong: toward helping to guide others along the path of their choice.

What then if you feel called to Interfaith ministry but don't yet know yourself? If that's the case, then before you embark on ministry, you need to find yourself. You need to know and be comfortable with who you are. How? Study, meditation, prayer, or perhaps counseling might be good places to begin. All of these, in combination or by themselves, can be valid ways of learning who we are. We should remember that despite

Hollywood and romance novels, who we are is rarely revealed to us in a magical moment of enlightenment. It takes time, effort, and intention. "Know thyself" is an injunction at least as old as the ancient Greeks and probably much older. It's worth the time for all of us, but it is particularly crucial if you seek to help others. I would add to that: "Know and be comfortable with thyself."

In case there's confusion, knowing and being comfortable with yourself does not mean that you stop growing or wanting to grow. If we stop growing, we die—spiritually if not literally. Nor does knowing and being comfortable with yourself, and particularly your shortcomings, mean that you're satisfied with where you are and have stopped trying to improve. What it does mean is that you understand and are comfortable with your own humanity even as you strive to be better. I believe it an important truth that recognizing and respecting our own humanity makes it a lot easier to recognize and respect the humanity of others.

Know at Least One Scripture Not Your Own (But Also Know Your Own)

I don't know how many truly bad movies, as well as a few good ones, have contained the line, "I lived with you all these years. But I never really knew you." The same may well be said of our relationship with Scripture. Many of us have lived with it for so long that we may not know what's actually there as well as we think we do. We know what we expect Scripture to say, and stop at that.

One of the most rewarding classes I had at the School of Theology and Ministry was "Hebrew Scripture." The reason it was so rewarding was that the class, in my opinion, was wrongly titled. It should have been called "An Introduction to Close Reading of Scripture." For me, one of the more challenging aspects about our Scriptures—Jewish, Christian, Muslim, Buddhist, and others—is that we are so accustomed to what we *expect* to find in them that we overlook that they have accumulated layer upon layer of interpretation. The idea behind Scriptural "close reading"[2] is to put aside all previous interpretations of a text—most particularly our own—and settle down to read and digest the text that is actually there. This, as many a student has found, can be a lot harder than it may appear. But it can also be enlightening.

I would strongly urge people interested in Interfaith ministry to reread closely their own Scripture, and then closely read the Scripture of at least one other spiritual path as well. A reason to closely read one's own Scripture is to learn just how many layers of interpretation there are as well as peel at least a few of them off. Only then is a potential minister in a position to begin to look at and appreciate the complexities of another path's sacred texts.

I think it's also beneficial to have real experience in two differing spiritual paths. It helps Interfaith ministers to create safe, sacred space if they understand the nature of sacred space from the perspective of at least two spiritual paths. Three would be better, but at least two.

If two are good and three are better, then why not six, eight, or ten? That's a question I've been asked. Indeed, I remember vividly being challenged once by a rather indignant fellow who demanded to know how I could call myself an interfaith minister—he considered Interfaith spiritual blasphemy—if I didn't know the Scriptures of all the spiritual paths. I think that's the other extreme, and in all honesty I don't think it's possible. But if we know and respect the Scripture of at least one or two spiritual paths that are not our own, I do believe it will help us to be far better guides.

Study

This gets tricky. A check of the Internet suggests a large number of places that appear to offer an interfaith education. But some of them seem to be nothing but ordination mills, offering a piece of paper with the title of "interfaith minister" yet little or no real preparation for the calling. I hope over time to visit as many institutions as I can and then report back. Check LivingInterfaith.org for updates on where to study to become an Interfaith minister. For me, there are some basic core studies, wherever you attend or choose to investigate on your own. Here are some key elements of an Interfaith ministry education:

1. A general introduction to the world's religions and how they developed.

2. Theology, even if one is an atheist! Theology is not the study of the truth about God but how humanity has thought about God.

3. A close reading of Scripture, which we've already discussed. This is not something that comes naturally.

4. Listening. This is a crucial if not *the* crucial aspect of what is called pastoral care. There is also something called the "Compassionate Listening Project," which I'd definitely recommend if a seminary class isn't available. Our culture teaches us how to argue. A minister needs to be able to listen.

5. Writing, with a focus on spiritual topics. What is important to talk about will vary from person to person, but how to organize those thoughts into a coherent form is a skill that takes practice.

6. Speaking, particularly about spiritual matters. In ministerial circles, this is sometimes called homiletics.

7. Personal reflection. We all lead busy lives. It is important, indeed crucial, to take some structured time to reflect on how and why we feel called to ministry.

I will try to update the Living Interfaith site (LivingInterfaith.org) frequently. And you can reach me with questions through that site. If Interfaith ministry calls to you, I wish you all the best. You are needed.

18

Anatomy of an Interfaith Service

You may or may not be interested in one day putting together your own Interfaith service. But if at some point you are, the how and, perhaps more important, the why of a Living Interfaith service may help clarify some of the intention needed to keep a service truly open and Interfaith.

Putting together an Interfaith service can require a lot of careful intention. The first question to be answered, of course, is why have a formal service at all? It's a good question. Whether they were intended that way or not, most formal services quickly evolve into an affirmation of "us." Formal services can be and frequently are exclusionary. I believe this is a big reason that many of us, myself included, have reacted negatively to some services, even and perhaps especially those offered by our own spiritual path.

So again, why would we want a formal service? One answer is that most of us like a little structure in our lives. Moreover, rituals can be both comforting and reassuring.

How then might we put together a service that has structure and ritual but also remains open and inclusive? That's where knowing what we want to accomplish and being intentional about it comes in and why it's so important. Perhaps the most straightforward way of looking at this is to examine the template of a Living Interfaith service.

There are whole books on how to put a service together. This is not one of them. I recall vast and sometimes complex lectures on theories in seminary. But I think it all comes down to this: A service is a chance to develop spiritual community. So a service should nourish our spirit and enhance our sense of community. Simple!

OK, a few nuts and bolts. For me, a service has three essential components, though how these components are framed is subject to endless variation. People are coming from their homes, their worlds if you will, so the first component is what is often called an "ingathering." An ingathering says, "Take a breath, settle in, we are coming together as a spiritual community."

The second component is the meat and potatoes—well, I'm vegetarian, so let's call it the veggies and carbohydrates. We come together as a community for spiritual nourishment, to feed our souls. We'll want to do things as a community: sing? have readings? pray? share? listen to a sermon? Any of these may have relevance in a given service.

The last component is the leave-taking. Having leave-taking as a component moves us away from the "Here's your hat—what's your hurry?" kind of ending. We not only want to send people out into the world again, but we also want to encourage them to take their sense of a loving community with them.

The guiding rationale behind a Living Interfaith service is that rituals are guides, not rules. Whatever we do must always aim at inclusion, not exclusion. We never want to simply pave over our differences. But always we want to respect our diversity, not simply tolerate it. I believe a worthwhile service will have ingathering, spiritual nourishment, and leave-taking. But what comprises these three elements may well vary greatly.

So that's the theory. What does this look like at Living Interfaith?

Ingathering

As folks walk in, we have name tags, both for regulars and visitors. A part of walking in is the ritual of putting on the name tag. Another part of walking in is passing a table with a large box labeled "Food Bank Donations." It is a reminder that we are indeed our brothers' and sisters' keepers, and we fill that box, sometimes to overflowing, at every service. Lastly, we set up a small bookcase for people to see as they come in. Here we keep Scriptures and other important texts from a multitude of spiritual paths, one right next to the other. They all share the same bookcase.

Our services then begin with a gentle piano prelude, followed by a verbal "Welcome." The welcome is there to set the tone of mutual respect for our diversity. What follows quickly became our weekly welcome.

> Welcome. Welcome to Living Interfaith. Know that the whole of you is welcome. You are not asked to leave who you are at the door. Bring who you are in with you. What you are asked to remember is that the people seated about you have also brought who *they* are in through the door as well. And all, *all* of goodwill are welcome.

Right. That's what we've come here for!

Next comes our opening prayer, Interfaith in its sensibility, followed by a hymn. This same hymn begins every service. It's in the hymnal for any who don't know it, and has long since been memorized by regulars. The hymn is based on the words of the Sufi poet Rumi. "Come, come whoever you are: wanderer, worshiper, lover of leaving. Ours is no caravan of despair. Come, yet again come."[1]

You may have noticed that our first song has reinforced that *all* are welcome.

There's the candlelighting,[2] a Passing of the Peace,[3] the requisite announcements, and then "Our Joint Affirmation" (page 125), an aspect of our service I believe is truly crucial. We say this together at every service.

The affirmation is, again, a broadly based reinforcement of our mutual respect. Ritual, it turns out, is important. The affirmation is not only an important and helpful ritual for those who come regularly, but it also reinforces gently yet clearly for any newcomers who we are. We are a welcoming community of diverse paths, who come together both to celebrate those paths and to work together to bring about a world of compassion, justice, and mutual respect.

With these words and intentions as our framework, we are ready to move from the ingathering to the core of the service. Our services are either built around a particular holiday from a specific spiritual path—holidays like Christmas, Passover, Ramadan, Bodhi Day, the Winter Solstice, among so many others—or an Interfaith theme—"Pondering Difficult Scripture," "Who Are You Bringing to the Witch-Burning?" "Gay Marriage: What's Really at Stake?" to name but a few.

But before proceeding, we need to pause for a moment. What follows is what we did for all our services through year 3. In year 4 we began to modify it. The difficulty is that our services were modeled after the service structure I was personally most familiar with, which is a Judeo-Christian structure. As you may remember, we started holding services a little faster than I had originally hoped, and to get things up and running I relied on what I knew. But the truth of it is that Buddhist, Muslim, Pagan, Baha'i, and other gatherings tend to be put together differently—some just a little, and some vastly.

What we ended up doing was having the same service structure for all spiritual paths. We invited a guest to share for twenty minutes during the sermon time, but the form for the rest of the service remained unchanged. I have come to understand and believe that this is not as welcoming to these diverse traditions as I'd hoped. Nor was it as respectful as I would want. In year 4, we began to follow our general service as outlined here if the tradition is Jewish or Christian in origin, or if we are following an Interfaith theme. But when, as example, the path we are honoring is Buddhism, we intentionally make the spiritual nourishment part of the service more reflective of that path. Among other things, that may mean sitting on cushions or pillows in a circle rather than in a semicircle of chairs around a pulpit.

Spiritual Nourishment

People are invited to share a particular passage of Scripture, literature, or a poem that calls to them spiritually. Always we preface these sharings by saying that we are not here to convert or convince. Rather, through these texts, poems, and expressions of our diverse spiritual paths we seek to share a bit of ourselves. It helps to make for a beautiful and worthwhile service. But it should also be noted that frequently no one shares a text. We hold the space open, but that is not a requirement. More important, I believe, the minister does not pick the readings, except on those rare occasions when I share a bit of myself. I tend to share a reading that is of particular importance to me personally perhaps three times a year.

We then sing an Interfaith response to the reading (even if there is no reading!). We are building up responses as we go, but at the moment we have Jewish, Muslim, Christian, Buddhist, Southwest Native American, and Pagan. We sing a different response at each service, whenever possible in keeping with the theme. As example, if we are honoring a Christian holy day, we sing the Doxology:

> *Praise God from whom all blessings flow.*
> *Praise God all creatures here below.*
> *Praise God above ye heavenly hosts.*
> *Praise Father, Son, and Holy Ghost.*

We then frequently have a responsive reading. As the minister, I choose this. It is directly related to the message and theme of the service, which means if we are honoring a specific spiritual path I pick the reading in consultation with whoever our guest speaker will be. I believe responsive readings are important as they "share the burden" of the reading. After the responsive reading, we sing a hymn before we share what is in our hearts. When we share our hearts, we share what's going on that is important to us, sometimes happy and sometimes not. This is not part of ingathering. It is spiritual nourishment. It helps us build community.

We then collect an offering because, well, we need money to operate! But at Living Interfaith we have introduced something important to me. I have been at any number of spiritual gatherings where a "plate" is passed. That means that you see what everyone else puts in and everyone else sees what you put in. I have personally always found that offensive. So we pass a small, lovely, cloth-lined basket that has a cover with a slot on top. No one can see or hear another's offering.

Then the choir sings, if there's a choir, and the congregation sings if there isn't. And then—drum roll, please—the minister or guest shares the morning's message. The message is usually about eighteen to twenty minutes long.

Leave-Taking

A final, uplifting hymn acts as a sort of "amen" for the message. We then gather in a circle. The minister says a few closing words that are intended to help the congregation transition from the formal service, and we sing a short song of community.

Then comes perhaps the most important part of any service: the social hour. Coffee, tea, and some edibles are provided and there is roughly one hour to chat. Sometimes what was offered in the morning's message causes further comment and other times people just catch up on what others have been doing. I believe that no spiritual gathering is truly of value unless we break bread together. I once thought this was a Jewish thing. But I've since learned it is a Muslim thing, and a Christian thing, and have come to understand it is a very human thing. There is something wonderfully sacred and spiritual to sharing food.

19

SOME INTERFAITH LITURGY

Here are some of the prayers, readings, and rituals that the Living Interfaith Church has created to be a part of our spiritual community. It is by no means comprehensive but it's a good place to start if you are looking for Interfaith material.

Our Joint Affirmation is spoken in unison at the beginning of every service.

Our Joint Affirmation

We come together in peace.
We sing together in joy and with love.
We worship together
In one house,
A house with names beyond number.

Our paths are many.
Our beliefs are as leaves.
And the tree that we cleave to
Is nourished by the light of
Compassion, justice, and mutual respect.

May our lives, our beliefs, and our actions
Help to bring about the world of love we all seek;
And let it begin here.

Responsive Readings

For any who may not be familiar with responsive readings, a reader usually stands at the front of the congregation. The reader's words are below in a regular font. The congregation then replies or responds with the words that are in italics.

The Interfaith Family

We are one;

One with our neighbor, with humanity, and with the universe.

We are all star stuff;

Every person, every frog, every tree, and every rock.

We gather, then, not to codify our perceived uniqueness;

But rather to celebrate our diversity—without fear or hierarchy.

Our differences are a cause for joy, not trembling.

As brothers and sisters, we need not look alike nor think alike to love one another.

May we always be guided by a respect for others as we respect ourselves, and the universe we all share.

May we be guided by compassion and community all the days of our lives.

The Overwhelming Call of We

Sometimes ... the world seems to come at me from all sides.

Sometimes ... I hurt, I hunger, I thirst, and I am filled with wanting.

Sometimes ... I forget that I am, I truly am, and I have a place in this Universe.

Sometimes ... I forget my value, and see only my faults.

At these times, I can tend to turn inward and see only myself.

At these times, I may see only my hurt, my thirst, my wants.

At these times I can forget you, my brother; and you, my sister.

At these times, my humanity ebbs.

Let me never forget that I am called not only to love and to compassion, but also to community.

And there is no community, if there is only me.

O, Hope of the Universe, we are all children of the universe.

Let us refuse to divide into camps of gender, "race," or spiritual path.

But let us come together.

May our lives be made richer and more whole by reaching out to one another, in times of joy and in times of terror.

May our lives be filled to overflowing by reaching out to one another.

Let us answer with unswerving faith, the overwhelming call of we.

I Release Myself from Anger

I release myself from anger.

I will not allow my heart or mind to become imprisoned.

I release myself from anger.

I choose to take a breath.

I release myself from anger.

I may not count to ten, but at least to four!

I release myself from anger.

I choose to remember that shouting will not make either of us any more or less right, only noisy.

I release myself from anger.

I choose not to hold my anger in, nor to aim it at others. Rather, I let it go.

I release myself from anger.

I choose to remember my humanity and yours.

The Gift of Meaning

Every molecule on earth, every atom of our bodies comes from the stars.

All that we are, all that we all are, is of the same solar soup.

We are all connected.

We are each and all of us star stuff.

My arm is related to your leg.

My heart is related to your brain.

We are all, inextricably intertwined.

If you have no meaning, then how can I?

If you are disposable, so am I.

If you are beloved, so am I.

We can mean together.

Or we can de-mean each other.

That we have a choice can be a gift or a curse.

Let our lives be a gift.

Prayers

Prayers are generally spoken by all in unison. But they might also be spoken by one person at the beginning of a service.

Bring Us Together

Bring us together.
We walk this one world
In different worlds.
Bring us together.

Help us see each other.
We tend to see what we expect,
Even when what we expect has fled.
Help us see each other.

If I need to stand upon your shoulders
To see across the field,
Let me not forget that you've a right
To stand on mine as well.

Let us "be" together.
Each ourselves
And yet as one united,
Let us "be" ... together.

Interfaith Prayer for Peace

May peace find a welcoming home in my heart.

May peace envelop me and flow through me in all that I embrace and all that I do.

May I be a beacon of peace.

And may I always remember that only a diversity of beacons can bring sufficient light to our paths to show us the way.

A Prayer for Forgiveness

Allow me to forgive,
For I am imprisoned by my bitterness.
Allow me to be forgiven,
For I am shamed that I have done another harm.

I earnestly pray that we may all forgive and be forgiven.
May we love and be loving.
May we strive to see the right, to do the right;
And to be generous with others as we would be with ourselves,
This day, this week, this life.

Amen.

Our Interfaith Prayer

We embrace our common humanity,
And acknowledge that we are all connected.

We embrace the compassion and love
That supports and nurtures our human community.

May we forgive, and be forgiven.
May we be accepting, and accepted.
May we be free from hunger and want,
As we strive to free our brothers and sisters from hunger and want.

May we always remember that
We are blessed by our blessing.
May we walk the sacred path of love,
By whatever branch that best guides us,
All the days of our lives.

New Member Ceremony

President:

Sometimes, membership in a group or an organization can become exclusionary. "We're in. You're not." Interfaith, as a faith, rejects the very essence of this "Us and Them" view of the world. No one is required to be a member. With the exception of voting for officers at the end of the year, there is no activity at Living Interfaith that a member may enjoy that a nonmember may not. Membership at Living Interfaith is about commitment, not about exclusion.

Will those who are signing the Membership book today please stand.

To take the step of membership is to commit to being an active part of Living Interfaith—its mission and vision. No one is asked to leave his or her spiritual path behind to join us. But *all* are asked to respect and honor each other as we come together to seek the world of love, compassion, and community that our spiritual paths, in their diversity, have called us to. Do you make such a commitment?

Signing Members:

We do.

President:

We are called as members of this church to covenant, to respect, nurture, and support all within this, our Interfaith community, founded upon compassionate action in the world. Do you freely accept and embrace this covenant in the name of love, that our children and their children may know a life of peace and justice, with the brotherhood and sisterhood that all of our faiths have taught us?

Signing Members:

We do.

President:

Will everyone present, members and friends alike, please stand. Are you witness to this covenant?

Congregation and Friends:

We are.

President (to signers):

Please sign our Membership book. (After each of the new members signs, they are given a certificate of membership. After all have signed, the minister welcomes them.)

Minister:

Welcome, welcome to Living Interfaith. Know that the whole of you is welcome.

Please be seated.

Baby/Child Dedication

This was written "on demand," when an Interfaith-oriented couple located out of state wrote me asking for help with their child dedication. Sometimes pressure is a good thing. I think this turned out rather well. And more important, the couple I sent it to appreciated it and used it. It is offered, again, as an example of the desire for inclusivity. It is not offered as the one right way to dedicate a baby or child.

Blessing

Leader (a minister, grandparent, or older friend of the family):

Please stand.

We come together from many roads and lives and spiritual pathways. We come together to share in welcoming this child into our world. At this sacred moment, we come to bless this child and to take from our very presence here a blessing of our own—a reminder that we are all connected, and that we are strengthened by that connection.

Response (All standing):

We affirm our common bond of love, compassion, and community. We affirm our common purpose of welcoming this child, this new life, this bundle of dreams and hope into the world.

Leader:

Please be seated.

I call upon the parents and any other children of this family to step forward with the newest member of our community.

[The parents and any children step forward]

[To the parents and children]

By what name shall we know this child?

Parents:

This is our son/daughter _____.

Children (if present):

This is our/my brother/sister _____.

Leader:

_____, your family welcomes you.

Please, each of you, share the breath of life with _____ [first name].

Mother and father and any children present, each, in turn, blows a gentle breath onto the child; each, in turn, then saying:

_____ I share with you my breath, my life. We are a family. We are each of us different and unique, and yet we are one family. I pledge to you my love as well as my breath. Welcome!

The leader calls the mother, father, and any children by name, then saying:

You are each individuals, and worthy of respect and celebration as individuals. And you are also a family, worthy of respect and celebration as a family. And you have welcomed _____ into your family with love and breath. May you always respect and celebrate one another.

The leader now turns to all others gathered:

We are a loving community as well. Each of us, while an individual, is an integral part of that community. Do you welcome _____ to be among you, in community?

Response:

We do.

Leader:

Will you support and help to nurture _____ as she/he grows, so that in receiving love and compassion, _____ may learn to be loving and compassionate?

Response:

We will.

Leader:

Our human community is diverse and grand. Our spiritual paths are diverse and grand. Will you celebrate and respect _____ in whatever spiritual path may call to him/her, so long as that path leads her/him to a life of love, compassion, and community?

Response:

We will.

Leader:

_____, welcome to the world. We are all so very pleased to greet you.

Response:

Amen.

Conclusion

WHERE DO WE GO FROM HERE?

I n *The Interfaith Alternative* a theological and historical case was made for Interfaith as a faith. In this book, we've examined the more practical aspects, answering the question, "What would Interfaith, as a faith, look like and how might we practice it?" As we conclude, the question becomes, "Now what?"

For the Living Interfaith Church, "Now what?" is more than simply continuing our twice-a-month services. We have come up with an ambitious, multiyear project to create an Interfaith educational curriculum that teaches children respect for other spiritual paths as well as laying a foundation for the parents' paths. Living Interfaith is committed not only to creating such a curriculum but also to making it available online and at no cost to any group that would like to use it. This is such a huge project that we've broken it down into four parts to make its creation possible. The overall project is to develop a curriculum for children and youth ages six through seventeen. We've begun Part 1, for ages six through eight. Once that's finished, we'll make it available on the web and then move on to do fund-raising for and then create Part 2, for ages nine through twelve.

But in the larger sense, what happens now is up to the reader. What is the world we want to live in? What is the world we want to bequeath to our children and grandchildren? And what are we willing to do about it? Since *The Interfaith Alternative* was published, I've been contacted by people from as far away as Great Britain, Italy, and Australia, as well as by a growing number of people across the United States and Canada. Some are interested in Interfaith but unsure of what to do about it. Others want to or already have started Interfaith communities and seek some guidance as well as moral support.

An even larger number of interfaith groups, not necessarily interested in Interfaith, still see much value simply in talking to one another. And they are right. There is indeed much value in that. I have no quarrel at all with interfaith. I simply seek to move beyond it.

My hope and my prayer is that these books will help to stimulate the creation of a multitude of welcoming Interfaith communities—circles, congregations, churches—all dedicated to creating safe, sacred space and celebrating our common humanity. But that is beyond my control. The ball now moves from my court to yours.

It has been an adventure writing and sharing *Practical Interfaith* with you, and I am glad to have had your company. And if you're ready—if you're willing to invest the effort—the adventure isn't over. In fact, the adventure is just beginning. We can change the world.

It's your turn now. Form a group. Share this book with others. Discuss it. Share your spiritual journeys. If and when you're ready, start an Interfaith community, a community that respects and celebrates the wondrous strands of our many spiritual paths. A few people at a time, little by little, we can nudge and encourage each other toward the grace and love we are all called to. Jew, Pagan, Christian, Muslim, Buddhist, Baha'i, Humanist, Hindu, First Peoples, and so many others—we are all called. The question that remains: Will we answer? After all these centuries, will we at last answer the call of the sacred to love and compassion?

Is it not time for the human family, at long, long last, to recognize our common humanity, even as we respect and honor our diversity? Is it not time to stop throwing rocks at each other and come together? And if it is, are you willing to help?

What do you say?

Appendix

POSSIBLY HELPFUL DOCUMENTS

B elow are some of the foundational materials for the Living Interfaith Church. They are offered, always, as guides, not doctrine; as examples, not dogma. Each is prefaced by a short introduction explaining its purpose. They are followed by our mission and vision statements, as well as our bylaws. Initially we didn't feel we needed mission and vision statements, let alone bylaws. But after our first three years we felt it important to crystallize not only who we were, but also to formalize how we would operate. We felt the time for seat-of-the-pants operation had passed. It was a good feeling.

Covenant and Assumptions

While we respect and honor our diverse spiritual paths, we weren't going to base our faith on any specific Scripture as definitive. So what was our foundation? What basic assumptions do we make about the world that bring us together? There were six assumptions that I felt needed to be stated. I also felt that we needed not only assumptions but also a covenant, an agreement among us, that we could fall back on in times of stress.

A group that became known as the Helping Hands (our board) met monthly to discuss these matters. As with everything, I submitted the covenant and assumptions to the Helping Hands for comment and reaction. Some changes were made. Below is the document we all agreed to.

Our Covenant and Six Fundamental Assumptions

We covenant to respect, nurture and support all within this our Interfaith community, founded upon compassionate action in the world. We base our covenant upon the following assumptions:

1) There is a spiritual core to the universe that calls us to our better selves if we will listen. Some may have a belief that this spiritual core is God and may have a clear belief as to who or what God is. Others may believe in a God who is less clearly defined. Still others may view this spiritual core in terms of a life-force or moral imperative, with no thought of God at all.

2) While each of us must define the meaning of our own lives, we understand, accept and embrace as self-evident that we are our brothers' and sisters' keeper, that we must strive daily to treat each other with honor, with respect and with love, and we recognize that this is what Jesus, Confucius, Hillel, the Buddha, Muhammad and so many others sought to teach us.

3) A part of that fundamental respect is to honor the multitude of spiritual paths that our fellow men and women have traveled and will travel.

4) We are defined by how we act and whom we help. We are called to act with compassion, love and respect not only within our community but within the entirety of the human community.

5) Economic, racial, ethnic, religious, gender, sexual orientation and all such divisions have no spiritual relevance, and any hierarchy based on them is both baseless and harmful.

6) The earth is our home, regardless of its creation history, and we are called upon to act as stewards and guardians of its wonders and diversity so that all generations may experience its profound beauty and richness to the fullest.

A Joint Declaration and Welcome

I felt it was important for us to have a common reading to begin our services. This reading would reinforce who we are, renew our covenant with each other and the world, and also help any visitor understand clearly what we are about. This was tweaked by the Helping Hands as well. It was a source of pleasure and affirmation that after the first year of services the declaration was considered such a foundational part of Living Interfaith that I was asked to copyright it. This is the same declaration that was included in our liturgy chapter.

Our Joint Declaration

We come together in peace.
We sing together in joy and with love.
We worship together
In one house,
A house with names beyond number.

Our paths are many.
Our beliefs are as leaves.
And the tree that we cleave to
Is nourished by the light of
Compassion, justice and mutual respect.

May our lives, our beliefs and our actions
Help to bring about the world of love we all seek;
And let it begin here.

Minister's Welcome

Welcome. Welcome to Living Interfaith. Know that the whole of you is welcome. You are not asked to leave who you are at the door. Bring who you are in with you. What you are asked to remember is that the people seated around you have brought who *they* are in with them as well. And all, *all* of goodwill are welcome.

Mission and Vision Statements

In our third year we drafted more formal documents. We put into writing our mission statement, our vision statement, and our bylaws. This was very much a group effort. We wrestled with these documents, particularly our bylaws, most of the year. But I believe the results were extraordinarily powerful. Bylaws, by the way, are essential if a group seeks to be recognized by the IRS as a charitable group. A church that raises money for church work does not need so-called charitable status. But we were ready to start applying for some grants. For that, we definitely wanted to have 501(c)(3) status.

Mission Statement

The purpose of the Living Interfaith Church is to provide a welcoming, respectful and nurturing religious community for people of goodwill from all spiritual paths. We share who we are and celebrate our diversity, not to convert or convince, but in realization of our common humanity. We aspire to offer a model of an inclusive community that acts as an agent of good works in the local community and the world.

Vision Statement

We envision our mission unfolding in such a way that we honor and welcome people from all spiritual paths, and covenant to encourage and empower each other as we root ourselves in social justice, in our own community and the world. We will establish a model for Interfaith education which truly respects the diversity that is humanity, and provide an example that other Interfaith congregations might follow without attachment to dogma—always keeping in mind that we are all worthy of respect, and our spiritual diversity is a cause for celebration.

Specifically:

Welcoming All Paths

Our mission is to provide a welcoming, respectful and nurturing home for people of goodwill from all spiritual paths. We seek to do so by creating:

1. Interfaith services that explore some of the ways our differing spiritual paths approach a question, and

2. Services that celebrate with integrity holy days from our differing spiritual paths, with the intent to share who we are, not to convert or convince.

We seek to do so by recognizing that it is not so much the beliefs we hold (which are deeply personal and to be respected) but how we act on those beliefs that is crucial—and that we are called by our common humanity to act with love, compassion, and respect in the world, always remembering that we are our brothers' and sisters' keepers.

Social Justice
Because we are brothers and sisters, an integral part of our vision is to act as a community to affirmatively address issues of social justice both at home and in the larger world. We also recognize and welcome the need to nurture and support each other as we act individually in the world as well. We understand and embrace that we are all unique, with different needs and skills, and therefore we will be called to engage the world differently. We keep centered in ourselves as individuals and as a group, that while we may indeed strive for great things, it is not the perceived magnitude of our accomplishments that defines us, but rather our commitment to community—to our own community, all of humanity and the natural world.

Interfaith Education
We seek to establish and employ a curriculum of Interfaith education that teaches to our children:

1. We are all beloved and deserving of love, and there is no one "right" path to this love;
2. We have differing spiritual roots and personal paths that need to be recognized, remembered and respected;
3. However beautiful and important our personal paths may be, it is crucial that we act in the world to promote our common humanity, to serve each other and with each other regardless of societal delineations based on gender, sexual orientation, race, nationality, religion, or economic circumstance—that no one is born into this world deserving of more or less love or respect than any other.

Interfaith Community
We seek to provide an example for other Interfaith congregations, not by expecting our answer to a specific question to be everyone else's, but by encouraging and promoting a multitude of Living Interfaith congregations, based on compassion, love and respect for all of humanity. Each congregation will be a welcoming home for all spiritual paths, so we may learn from each other, and celebrate with each other our differences as well as our

similarities, with dignity and respect. We hope to be a template for how we can engage our own spiritual nature, not by finding one "right path" to it, but by truly learning to get to know each other [and at last both find and realize what all of our spiritual paths have taught us: we share a common humanity].

Our Bylaws

Bylaws, by their very nature, have some legalistic and, let's face it, rather boring sides to them. But they are essential because bylaws provide a framework for how the church will function. While they can sometimes be a bother, bylaws are there to prevent a haphazard approach to how the church is run. But more than that, we also wanted our bylaws to reflect who we are. It took months to get this right. We discussed, polished, and tweaked. Below is what we came up with. We put our bylaws (as well as our other documents) on our website, in part so that people wouldn't feel that they needed to reinvent the wheel. We also annotated them (annotations in brackets below) in a couple of key spots to point out the "why" of that particular bylaw.

Living Interfaith Church Bylaws

[Article One is fairly standard. Note that 1.1 mentions we are a nonprofit religious organization: This clearly states that our intent is to be a church, NOT a "for profit" group that happens to deal with religious themes; 1.3 is a legal requirement—a nonprofit has to have a defined way of transferring any remaining assets to another nonprofit.]

Article One: Name

1.1.   The name of our non-profit religious organization is LIVING INTERFAITH CHURCH.

1.2.   The location of Living Interfaith Church is Lynnwood, Washington.

1.3.   In the event of a dissolution of this corporation, any assets of the congregation will be transferred to the Interfaith Association of Northwest Washington, (a recognized 501(c)(3) corporation), located in Everett, WA, or its successor organization, for its general purposes; this transfer to be made in full compliance with applicable law.

Article Two: Statement of Purpose

2.1. Notwithstanding any other provisions of these Bylaws, Living Interfaith Church shall not carry on any activities not permitted to be carried on by a corporation exempt from federal income tax under Section 501(c)(3) of the Internal Revenue code.

[*This is required by the IRS if an organization wants to become a recognized 501(c)(3) charity.*]

2.2. Living Interfaith Church is a non-profit religious organization whose purpose is to hold regular services, encourage and support members in their individual religious and spiritual growth and expression, and to further the growth of Interfaith as a faith in the world. Living Interfaith Church is an inclusive interfaith ministry.

2.3. This congregation affirms and promotes the full participation of persons in our activities and endeavors, including membership, programming, hiring practices, and the calling of religious professionals without regard to gender, affectional or sexual orientation, race, ethnicity, nationality, religion, physical or mental challenge, or economic circumstance.

2.4. Any limitation to full participation is subject to review and approval by the Church Council.

2.5. In putting our purpose into practice, we shall design all our activities, programs, celebrations, and community work such that we constantly evaluate and consider how what we do affects everyone else, both within our church community and in the broader community.

2.6. A "Statement of Rationale," which will document the reasoning underlying our Bylaws and the motivating force behind our Policies and Procedures, shall serve as a fixed preamble to the current and any future Policies and Procedures so that the initial intent remains clear, even as the Bylaws and Policies and Procedures are amended.

[*We decided we wanted a "Statement of Rationale" as a "fixed preamble" to our Policies and Procedures so that, despite any changes in those policies and procedures that might be made in the future, all in the future will know what we intended.*]

Article Three: Membership

3.1.   Membership privileges as defined in these Bylaws will be extended only to Active Members. An Active Member is any person who:

3.1.1. Is 16 years of age or older; and

3.1.2. Has completed the Journey to Membership process as outlined in the Membership Handbook of Living Interfaith Church; and

3.1.3. Makes an annual financial pledge of record toward the expenses of the organization; and

3.1.4. Has been accepted by a majority vote of the Church Council; and

3.1.5. Has signed the Membership book signifying his/her sympathy with the Covenant, current Bylaws and Mission Statement of Living Interfaith Church.

3.2.   One may be an Active Member of Living Interfaith Church and also be an active member of another spiritual community. Membership in our church is neither intended nor expected to be exclusive. No member is asked to give up his or her path in another spiritual community to join Living Interfaith Church. Rather, one is invited to broaden that path.

[This was and is considered a crucial part of our bylaws. We wanted to be clear that a person is not required to leave another spiritual path to join ours. We are a "both/and" and NOT an "either/or" church.]

Article Four: The Church Council

4.1.   The Church Council is the board of trustees of Living Interfaith Church. It is responsible for the well-being and care of the life, work and people of the church community and, more specifically, for all programs, celebrations and events. It is additionally responsible for all personnel, buildings, property and finances of the church community.

4.2.   All actions of Living Interfaith Church are to be transparent. Council meetings are open to the community and everyone is encouraged to attend. There may be instances where, for confidentiality reasons, a meeting or a portion of a meeting may be considered closed. This shall be constituted as an Executive

Session and will be open to only to voting Council Members and any individuals specifically requested to attend. The attending Council Members shall make the determination that an Executive Session should be invoked. Only actions and decisions of an Executive Session will be recorded in the minutes.

4.3. The Church Council is composed of an even number of elected members of Living Interfaith Church plus the Minister. Any Active Member of the congregation is eligible to be elected to the Council.

4.4. The Council will normally hold its regular meetings once a month, on the 3rd Saturday of the month, but shall not hold these meetings less frequently than once per quarter. Any Council Member may call special meetings when necessary.

4.5. Members of the Church Council shall conduct themselves according to the Covenant of Right Relations detailed in the Church Administrative Policy and Procedures.

4.6. Members of the Church Council shall serve without compensation.

4.7. All members of the Church Council, and any persons acting on behalf of Living Interfaith Church, shall abide by the church policy regarding Conflict of Interest as detailed in the church Policies and Procedures, which shall conform to current law and standards.

Article Five: Nomination and Election to the Church Council

5.1. Church Council and interested volunteers from the church community will constitute the Nominating Committee for new members of the Council.

5.2. Only persons who are Active Members of Living Interfaith Church as defined in Article Three of these Bylaws and in the Policies and Procedures and who meet the Membership requirements of the Church may be nominated and elected to the Church Council.

5.3. Only Active Members of Living Interfaith Church as defined in the Article Three of these Bylaws shall have voting privileges in Church elections and/or Congregational meetings.

5.4. Persons are elected to the Church Council for a one-year term.

5.5. If at any time during a Church Council member's term, he or she becomes unable to fulfill her or his commitment to the Church Council, he or she may request a leave of absence or submit a letter of resignation. Church Council members will notify the President of the Church Council if they are unable to attend a meeting. If, in the absence of extenuating circumstances, Church Council members fail to attend three consecutive Church Council meetings, it will be considered that they have resigned and their position will be filled by the Council for the remainder of the unexpired terms.

Article Six: Officers of the Church

6.1. The officers of Living Interfaith Church are the President, Vice-President, Secretary, and Treasurer. All officers may be considered for re-election up to but not exceeding four (4) years.

6.2. Officers are elected at the Annual Meeting of the Church Council.

6.3. The President of the Church Council is directly responsible for the ongoing work of the Church Council. The President of the Church Council works in direct relationship with the Minister, members of the Council, and the church community. The agenda for Council meetings is set by the President in conjunction with the Minister. The President is authorized to transact business in the name of the corporation, so long as such business is approved by the Council.

6.4. The Vice-President of the Church Council assists the President as directed by the President and serves as a liaison to the church community. The Vice-President presides at Council meetings in the President's absence.

6.5. The Treasurer functions as a full member of the Council and works in direct relationship with the Minister, the President of the Council and the Bookkeeper. The Treasurer is responsible for maintaining accurate financial records, all financial disbursements, and for continuous awareness of the income and expenses of the church.

6.6. The Secretary functions as a full member of the Council and works in direct relationship with the Minister and the President of the Council. The Secretary shall keep accurate minutes of all Council meetings and any Congregational meeting, and if the Secretary cannot be present the Secretary shall secure a substitute.

6.7. Any Officer may be removed either with or without cause by supermajority two-thirds (2/3, 66%) vote of the Church Council at any time.

6.8. All meetings will be conducted according to the Administrative Policies and Procedures and Robert's Rules of Order Newly Revised, provided such procedures are applicable and not inconsistent with these Bylaws.

Article Seven: Minister

7.1. The Minister is responsible to the Church Council and works in direct relationship with the President of the Church Council. The Minister is responsible for coordinating the various aspects of ministry within the perspective of the total life and ministry of Living Interfaith Church.

7.2. The Minister is a member of the Living Interfaith Church. The Minister's performance, salary, and benefits are reviewed no less than once a year by the Council and/or the designated Ministry Review Committee during the development of the new fiscal year's budget. Any recommended changes are submitted to the Church Council with the budget for approval.

7.3. If the Review or exigent circumstance indicates that a situation may require a change in the occupant of the position of Minister, the Council and Ministry Review Committee shall discuss the matter with the Minister present, and shall work out a course of action satisfactory to all parties. Should this not be possible, and should a supermajority of two-thirds (2/3, 66%) of the Council vote that the Minister be dismissed, the Council shall call a special meeting of the Congregation to vote on dismissal or retention of the Minister. A two-thirds (2/3) vote of the Congregation shall be required to dismiss the Minister.

7.4. In the event of the Minister's termination or resignation from the position, the Council will create an Interim Ministry of volunteers from among the Membership to maintain regular services while a Search Committee is convened by the Council. The Council shall make every effort to retain a new permanent Minister within one year of the departure of the previous Minister. If a new minister is not identified within that time, the Council will hold a meeting to consult with the congregation on next steps.

Article Eight: Committees

8.1. The Church Council may create and define various regular committees and ad hoc committees as needed. These committees will report regularly to the Church Council and the Church Council may disband the committees when their function is no longer needed.

Article Nine: Decisions and Procedures

9.1. Because Living Interfaith Church is a Community, decisions at meetings of the Church Council and the Congregation will be made by consensus.

[We decided early on that we wanted, if at all possible, to use a consensus model rather than simply "vote." Consensus takes longer. But our feeling was that we wanted to really talk things through, understand why consensus couldn't be reached—when that's the case—and work on it until consensus could be reached. Thus far we have always reached consensus. However, below are provisions for what to do when/if consensus cannot be reached.]

9.2. Where consensus cannot be reached at Council meetings in a reasonable period of time, an open or private vote may be called by agreement of the majority of Council members where a quorum is present. In that event, decisions will be made by an affirmative vote of a majority of Council members present to be conducted according to Robert's Rules of Order Newly Revised.

9.3. Where consensus cannot be reached at Congregational meetings in a reasonable period of time, an open or private vote may be called by agreement of the majority of Active Members where a quorum is present. In that event, decisions will be made by an affirmative vote of a simple majority of Active Members present per Robert's Rules of Order Newly Revised.

9.4. Once a decision is made that consensus cannot be reached, all Council and Congregational meetings shall be conducted according to Robert's Rules of Order Newly Revised, provided such procedures are applicable and not inconsistent with these Bylaws.

9.5. The Council will develop, and annually review prior to the Annual Congregational Meeting, a document of Administrative Policies and Procedures to govern all functions of the Church not covered by these Bylaws, the Financial Policies and Procedures, and the Membership Handbook. In situations where a course of action is unclear, the actions of the Council will be determined by these Policies and Procedures. These documents and any changes to them will be presented at the Congregational Meeting (described in Section 10 of these Bylaws) for approval by a simple majority of Active Members present, and approved by Council vote as stated in Sections 9.1 and 9.2 above.

9.6. In keeping with church policy of transparency, accurate records shall be kept:

9.6.1. Minutes of all meetings of the Church Council and any Council-sanctioned committees and Congregational meetings shall be kept, indicating the time and place of such meetings, the names of those present, and actions and decisions made by the Council during the meeting.

9.6.2. Accurate financial records of the Church shall be kept, including receipts and disbursements.

9.6.3. A record of Active Members shall be kept and updated at least once a year, before each Annual Congregational Meeting.

9.6.4. The Church Council shall cause any annual or periodic report required by law to be prepared and delivered to an office of the State of Washington or the IRS in a timely manner.

Article Ten: Congregational Meetings

10.1. An Annual Congregational Meeting will be held at or near the end of the Church fiscal year. Twenty-five percent (25%) of the Active Membership, except as otherwise noted, shall constitute a quorum. Meetings shall be governed by the provisions set out in the Bylaws.

10.2. A notice of the time, date and location of the Annual Congregational meeting shall be announced in the Sunday program for two consecutive services preceding the meeting.

10.3. Any Active Member may request an item be added to the Agenda of the Annual Meeting by presenting such request in writing to the Council President at any time prior to the meeting.

10.4. In addition to the Annual Congregational Meeting, the Church Council may, when needed, call a Congregational Meeting comprised of all the members of the Church community. Normally, these meetings will take place on Sunday, following the service. Whenever possible, the congregation will be given two weeks advance notice of such meetings. The President or Vice-President of the Church Council or the Minister (or designee) will moderate such meetings.

10.5. Congregational Meetings may also be called by petition presented to the Church Secretary, containing the signatures of at least twenty-five percent (25%) of the Active Members to discuss items stated in the petition.

Article Eleven: Amendments, Additions, and Deletions to Bylaws

11.1. These Bylaws may be modified with amendments, additions, or deletions, by an affirmative vote made by two-thirds (2/3) of the Active Members in attendance at the annual meeting of the Congregation.

11.2. At least fourteen days prior to the Annual Congregational meeting, the Members shall be notified by mail with a summary of the proposed changes to the Bylaws and of their opportunity to receive a copy of the complete text of the proposed changes. The complete text of the proposed changes shall be available to any member requesting it.

11.3. Only Active Members may propose an amendment, addition or deletion. A member must first present the proposal, in writing, to the Church Council. The Church Council must approve changes to the Bylaws before they are presented to the members, except as provided for below.

11.4. A proposed change to the Bylaws may be presented at the Annual Congregational meeting, contrary to the prior expressed desire of Church Council, if such proposal is presented attached to a petition signed by fifty-one percent (51%) of the active church Membership. Such petition must be presented to any Council member 30 days prior to the Annual Congregational meeting.

Article Twelve: Indemnification and Non-liability

12.1. Living Interfaith Church shall indemnify its Council Members and Officers to the fullest extent permissible under the laws of this state from any claim of damage or liability against them while acting in good faith on behalf of the Church.

12.2. The Council Members shall not be personally liable for the debts, liabilities, or other obligations of Living Interfaith Church.

NOTES

1 Interfaith as a Faith

1. Paul McKenna at the Scarboro Missions, near Toronto, Canada, has dedicated much of his life to spreading the word about the universality of the Golden Rule. More about his profound and beautiful Golden Rule poster and materials may be found at www.scarboromissions.ca. They are well worth exploring and a great teaching aid.

2. For a much fuller discussion about this, see my previous book, *The Interfaith Alternative: Embracing Spiritual Diversity* (Gabriola Island, BC: New Society Publishers, 2012), which focuses extensively on this difficult question.

3 Why Are Our Spiritual Paths So Different?

1. See *The Interfaith Alternative,* pp. 7–12, 25–30.

4 What We Call It Matters

1. For a fuller discussion, see *The Interfaith Alternative,* pp. 85–88.

2. About two years ago I experienced just such a dialogue. I answered my doorbell to find a friendly young man waiting to engage me. He introduced himself as a local minister and asked, "Are you churched?" I replied that not only was I "churched" but I, too, was a minister. He asked what denomination I was. I informed him I was an Interfaith minister. After I told him what that meant, he gave me a big smile. He said, "You do realize you are going to hell." He then pivoted and walked away. So, "I'm right and you're going to hell" is still alive and well in the twenty-first century.

3. *Nostra Aetate* denies the centuries-old accusation that the Jewish people were collectively guilty of killing Jesus, stresses the religious bond shared by Jews and Catholics, reaffirms the eternal covenant between God and the children of Israel, and dismisses church interest in trying to baptize Jews. It was also the first church document to call for Catholics and Jews to engage in dialogue to better understand each other's faith. See Anti-Defamation League,

"The Nostra Aetate: What Is It?"; http://archive.adl.org/main_interfaith/nostra_aetate_whatisit.html#.U6hyYMvD-M9 (accessed June 23, 2014).

6 The Decision to Act

1. It is also helpful to remember that while Interfaith frees us to walk the spiritual path of our choosing, it does not release us from a need to find that path, a path that will enable us to be a more loving and compassionate member of the human community, and then to walk it.
2. It will take practice—a lot of it. Most of us will stumble along the way. As long as we are willing to acknowledge our stumbling and continue to practice our Interfaith, that is what is important.

7 Why Interfaith Can Be Hard

1. *What's Wrong with the World* (Seven Treasures Publications, 2009). This is frequently paraphrased as "Christianity has not been tried and found wanting; it has been found difficult and not tried."
2. For much more about this unfortunate paradigm, see *The Interfaith Alternative*, pp. 3–55.
3. I've often pondered why there are so many reality shows on television based on judging. Judge Alex, Judge Judy, Judge Whomever. And, of course, shows like those of Jerry Springer and Maury Povich. I have a feeling that a major reason they are so popular may be because they invite us to judge others and find them inferior.

8 What Does It Mean to Practice Interfaith?

1. "Remarks on East-West Relations at the Brandenburg Gate in West Berlin"; the Reagan Library, June 12, 1987.
2. *Gleanings from the Writings of Baha'u'llah* (quoted in *World Scripture* [New York: Paragon House, 1991], p. 188).
3. *Adi Granth*, Japuji 28 (quoted in *World Scripture*, p. 188).
4. Quoted in *World Scripture*, p. 189.
5. Frank Herbert, *Dune* (New York: Ace Books, 1987), p. 8.
6. If you've never seen the lovely Bob Newhart riff on this, check out YouTube and search for "Newhart Stop It."

9 The Foundation of Interfaith Dialogue

1. Parker J. Palmer, *A Hidden Wholeness: The Journey toward an Undivided Life* (Hoboken, NJ: Jossey-Bass, 2004). Palmer does a truly wonderful job of presenting both why establishing a circle of trust is so important and how it can be done. There is more to his book than merely teaching us how to form a circle of trust, and I found the entire book worthwhile. But even if

you only read it to grasp more fully the nature of a circle of trust, I believe it will be well worth your time.

2. There are two books that I would strongly suggest to have available for reading alongside this one. One, if you'll forgive me, is my first book: *The Interfaith Alternative.* It can help provide both insight and a common language for further discussions of interfaith and Interfaith. Common language is much too often overlooked. But if, as example, you and I are going to talk about God, isn't it important for us to truly understand what each of us means by that word? The other book that I would recommend is Parker Palmer's *A Hidden Wholeness*, especially pp. 51–87.

11 Holding Safe, Sacred Space

1. A quick word of warning: Historical linguistics, something I studied in college, is an inexact science. Word origins can be tricky. We can make educated guesses as to how and why a word changed both its spelling and its meaning. Some word origins are much clearer than others. But since we weren't there, very frequently we can't know for sure. The *Oxford English Dictionary* spends a good deal of time trying to find the answer. Does "church" come from the Greek "kyriake"? Does it come from the Old English "cirice" or "circe"? Did the Old English "cirice" become "kirche" become "church"? No one knows.

2. More about this in chapter 15, "Some Thoughts on Interfaith Ministry."

12 Foundations for Starting an Interfaith Spiritual Community

1. In *The Interfaith Alternative.* I talk at length about the toxic and isolating effect that right belief—the notion that there is one and only one right belief about God and the sacred—has had on human history.

2. A dear friend astonished me many years ago when he told me he belonged to the Jim Smith Club. The common factor is, well, that every member's name is Jim Smith. And, folks, the club is huge!

13 The Road to Living Interfaith

1. Very recently, I came upon this wonderful quote from the late African-American feminist Audre Lorde. She wrote, "It is not our differences that divide us. It is our inability to recognize, accept, and celebrate those differences." Amen, sister!

2. One of the poems I wrote as a child held the refrain, "Sing me not of word, but deed."

3. Arberry's Qur'an translation (A. J. Arberry, *The Koran Interpreted: A Translation* [Touchstone, 1996]).

14 Joys and Bumps along the Way

1. Our Bylaws do provide procedures on actually taking a vote. But so far this
   has never been necessary. And, yes, it would be more helpful here if I could
   recount what the issues were that took three or more meetings to resolve.
   But I honestly don't remember them. That's how low-key and unheated we
   keep the discussions.

Resources for an Interfaith Community

1. A favorite book of mine is *For Praying Out Loud: Interfaith Prayers for Public
   Occasions* by L. Annie Foerster. While the book does have its limitations, it
   is a wonderful resource and I recommend it.

16 Choosing an Interfaith Minister

1. For the sake of simplicity, I include under the title "minister" priests and
   rabbis. For me a minister is one who "ministers" to the spiritual needs of a
   congregation.
2. At some point, we'll undoubtedly need Interfaith-specific terms for clergy.
   At this moment, I lean toward referring to our ministers as Brother or Sister,
   and perhaps describing their work as that of a spiritual guide rather than, as
   example, a pastor. Personally, neither I nor my congregation thinks of me as
   a shepherd.

17 I Think I Want to Be an Interfaith Minister

1. If the urge to compare Interfaith with other faiths becomes irresistible, please
   do remember that every faith has started small. Christianity, as example,
   which has spread throughout the globe, began as a very small movement,
   with congregations gathering in people's homes and no paid ministry.
2. At least as defined by my professor Father James Eblen. James and I would
   part ways over a foundational disagreement about Interfaith, but I shall
   always remain grateful to him for his class on close reading.

18 Anatomy of an Interfaith Service

1. This is from the Unitarian Universalist hymnal, *Singing the Living Tradition*
   (Boston: Unitarian Universalist Association, 1993), which is the hymnal we
   use a majority of the time. There are some profound limitations to the UU
   hymnal, not the least of which is a lack of respect for traditional Christian
   hymns. But for all its weaknesses, it is the closest thing to an Interfaith
   hymnal, at least until we have enough funding to publish our own hymnal.
2. OK, we meet in a school cafeteria, with no flames allowed. So we use wax
   facades with LED lights.

3. With a reminder to respect each other's space, as some of us are huggers and some of us aren't, we stand and greet each other one by one. It is suggested that the first to speak says, "Peace be unto you." It is suggested that the reply be, "And also to you." These are only suggestions, as the point is not the words but the intent. The idea is borrowed from my experience in several Christian churches. There is something powerful about looking each other in the eyes and wishing one another peace.

SUGGESTIONS FOR FURTHER READING

Basic Works

To read along with or immediately after *Practical Interfaith*.

Greenebaum, Steven. *The Interfaith Alternative: Embracing Spiritual Diversity.* Gabriola Island, BC: New Society Publishers, 2012.

Palmer, Parker J. *A Hidden Wholeness: The Journey Toward an Undivided Life.* San Francisco: Jossey-Bass, 2009.

Interfaith Texts and Scripture

Novak's work is meant to be read; Wilson's is more of a resource in searching for how our differing paths approach a particular topic. I use *World Scripture* a lot.

Novak, Philip. *The World's Wisdom: Sacred Texts of the World's Religions.* New York: HarperOne, 1995.

Wilson, Andrew, ed. *World Scripture: A Comparative Anthology of Sacred Texts.* New York: Paragon House, 1998.

Interfaith Dialogue

Getting to the Heart of Interfaith and *Jewish Christian Dialogue* are "must reads"; *Interfaith Dialogue and Peacebuilding* is quite interesting, but somewhat academic. *Acts of Faith* is Patel's very personal journey to an interfaith approach.

Boys, Mary C. *Jewish Christian Dialogue: One Woman's Experience.* New York: Paulist Press, 1997.

Mackenzie, Don, Ted Falcon, and Jamal Rahman. *Getting to the Heart of Interfaith: The Eye-Opening, Hope-Filled Friendship of a Pastor, a Rabbi and an Imam.* Woodstock, VT: SkyLight Paths Publishing, 2009.

Patel, Eboo. *Acts of Faith: The Story of an American Muslim, the Struggle for the Soul of a Generation*. Boston: Beacon Press, 2010.

Smoch, David R., ed. *Interfaith Dialogue and Peacebuilding*. Washington, DC: U.S. Institute of Peace Press, 2002.

Our Diverse Spiritual Paths

A New Religious America is a thorough yet readable account of encountering the immense diversity that is the American scene. *Divinity and Diversity* is a readable approach to diversity by a Christian theologian. *A New Handbook of Living Religions* is thorough, somewhat dry, and rather academic but, that said, it is also a wonderful and comprehensive look at the diverse religions that are currently practiced in the world. Note: "Living" religions—religions that may once have been important but are no longer practiced—are not included.

Eck, Diana L. *A New Religious America: How a "Christian Country" Has Become the World's Most Religiously Diverse Nation*. New York: HarperSanFrancisco, 2002.

Hinnells, John, ed. *A New Handbook of Living Religions*. New York: Penguin Books, 2003.

Suchocki, Marjorie Hewitt. *Divinity and Diversity: A Christian Affirmation of Religious Pluralism*. Nashville: Abingdon Press, 2003.

Inspiration

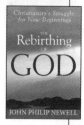

The Rebirthing of God
Christianity's Struggle for New Beginnings
By John Philip Newell
Drawing on modern prophets from East and West, and using the holy island of Iona as an icon of new beginnings, Celtic poet, peacemaker and scholar John Philip Newell dares us to imagine a new birth from deep within Christianity, a fresh stirring of the Spirit.
6 x 9, 160 pp, HC, 978-1-59473-542-4 **$19.99**

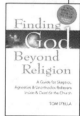

Finding God Beyond Religion: A Guide for Skeptics, Agnostics & Unorthodox Believers Inside & Outside the Church
By Tom Stella; Foreword by The Rev. Canon Marianne Wells Borg
Reinterprets traditional religious teachings central to the Christian faith for people who have outgrown the beliefs and devotional practices that once made sense to them.
6 x 9, 160 pp, Quality PB, 978-1-59473-485-4 **$16.99**

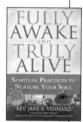

Fully Awake and Truly Alive: Spiritual Practices to Nurture Your Soul
By Rev. Jane E. Vennard; Foreword by Rami Shapiro
Illustrates the joys and frustrations of spiritual practice, offers insights from various religious traditions and provides exercises and meditations to help us become more fully alive.
6 x 9, 208 pp, Quality PB, 978-1-59473-473-1 **$16.99**

Journeys of Simplicity: Traveling Light with Thomas Merton, Bashō, Edward Abbey, Annie Dillard & Others *By Philip Harnden*
Invites you to consider a more graceful way of traveling through life. PB includes journal pages to help you get started on your own spiritual journey.
5½ x 7¼, 144 pp, Quality PB, 978-1-59473-181-5 **$12.99**
5½ x 7¼, 128 pp, HC, 978-1-893361-76-8 **$16.95**

Perennial Wisdom for the Spiritually Independent
Sacred Teachings—Annotated & Explained
Annotation by Rami Shapiro; Foreword by Richard Rohr
Weaves sacred texts and teachings from the world's major religions into a coherent exploration of the five core questions at the heart of every religion's search.
5½ x 8½, 336 pp, Quality PB Original, 978-1-59473-515-8 **$16.99**

Saving Civility: 52 Ways to Tame Rude, Crude & Attitude for a Polite Planet
By Sara Hacala
Provides fifty-two practical ways you can reverse the course of incivility and make the world a more enriching, pleasant place to live.
6 x 9, 240 pp, Quality PB, 978-1-59473-314-7 **$16.99**

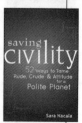

Spiritually Healthy Divorce: Navigating Disruption with Insight & Hope
By Carolyne Call
A spiritual map to help you move through the twists and turns of divorce.
6 x 9, 224 pp, Quality PB, 978-1-59473-288-1 **$16.99**

Or phone, fax, mail or email to: SKYLIGHT PATHS Publishing
Sunset Farm Offices, Route 4 • P.O. Box 237 • Woodstock, Vermont 05091
Tel: (802) 457-4000 • Fax: (802) 457-4004 • www.skylightpaths.com
Credit card orders: (800) 962-4544 (8:30AM–5:30PM EST Monday–Friday)
Generous discounts on quantity orders. SATISFACTION GUARANTEED. Prices subject to change.

Judaism / Christianity / Islam / Interfaith

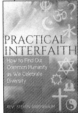

Practical Interfaith: How to Find Our Common Humanity as We Celebrate Diversity *By Rev. Steven Greenebaum*
Explores Interfaith as a faith—and as a positive way to move forward. Offers a practical, down-to-earth approach to a more spiritually fulfilling life.
6 x 9, 160 pp (est), Quality PB, 978-1-59473-569-1 **$16.99**

Sacred Laughter of the Sufis: Awakening the Soul with the Mulla's Comic Teaching Stories & Other Islamic Wisdom
By Imam Jamal Rahman
The legendary wisdom stories of Islam's great comic foil with spiritual insights for seekers of all traditions—or none.
6 x 9, 192 pp, Quality PB, 978-1-59473-547-9 **$16.99**

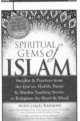

Spiritual Gems of Islam: Insights & Practices from the Qur'an, Hadith, Rumi & Muslim Teaching Stories to Enlighten the Heart & Mind
By Imam Jamal Rahman
Invites you—no matter what your practice may be—to access the treasure chest of Islamic spirituality and use its wealth in your own journey.
6 x 9, 256 pp, Quality PB, 978-1-59473-430-4 **$16.99**

Religion Gone Astray: What We Found at the Heart of Interfaith
By Pastor Don Mackenzie, Rabbi Ted Falcon and Imam Jamal Rahman
Welcome to the deeper dimensions of interfaith dialogue—exploring that which divides us personally, spiritually and institutionally.
6 x 9, 192 pp, Quality PB, 978-1-59473-317-8 **$16.99**

Getting to the Heart of Interfaith: The Eye-Opening, Hope-Filled Friendship of a Pastor, a Rabbi & an Imam *By Pastor Don Mackenzie, Rabbi Ted Falcon and Imam Jamal Rahman*
6 x 9, 192 pp, Quality PB, 978-1-59473-263-8 **$16.99**

Hearing the Call across Traditions: Readings on Faith and Service
Edited by Adam Davis; Foreword by Eboo Patel
6 x 9, 352 pp, Quality PB, 978-1-59473-303-1 **$18.99**

Blessed Relief: What Christians Can Learn from Buddhists about Suffering
By Gordon Peerman 6 x 9, 208 pp, Quality PB, 978-1-59473-252-2 **$16.99**

Christians & Jews—Faith to Faith: Tragic History, Promising Present, Fragile Future *By Rabbi James Rudin*
6 x 9, 288 pp, HC, 978-1-58023-432-0 **$24.99***   Quality PB, 978-1-58023-717-8 **$18.99***

Christians & Jews in Dialogue: Learning in the Presence of the Other *By Mary C. Boys and Sara S. Lee; Foreword by Dorothy C. Bass* 6 x 9, 240 pp, Quality PB, 978-1-59473-254-6 **$18.99**

InterActive Faith: The Essential Interreligious Community-Building Handbook
Edited by Rev. Bud Heckman with Rori Picker Neiss; Foreword by Rev. Dirk Ficca
6 x 9, 304 pp, Quality PB, 978-1-59473-273-7 **$16.99**; HC, 978-1-59473-237-9 **$29.99**

The Jewish Approach to God: A Brief Introduction for Christians
By Rabbi Neil Gillman, PhD 5½ x 8½, 192 pp, Quality PB, 978-1-58023-190-5 **$16.95***

The Jewish Approach to Repairing the World (Tikkun Olam): A Brief Introduction for Christians *By Rabbi Elliot N. Dorff, PhD, with Rev. Cory Willson*
5½ x 8½, 256 pp, Quality PB, 978-1-58023-349-1 **$16.99***

The Jewish Connection to Israel, the Promised Land: A Brief Introduction for Christians *By Rabbi Eugene Korn, PhD* 5½ x 8½, 192 pp, Quality PB, 978-1-58023-318-7 **$14.99***

Jewish Holidays: A Brief Introduction for Christians *By Rabbi Kerry M. Olitzky and Rabbi Daniel Judson* 5½ x 8½, 176 pp, Quality PB, 978-1-58023-302-6 **$18.99***

Jewish Ritual: A Brief Introduction for Christians
By Rabbi Kerry M. Olitzky and Rabbi Daniel Judson 5½ x 8½, 144 pp, Quality PB, 978-1-58023-210-4 **$14.99***

Jewish Spirituality: A Brief Introduction for Christians *By Rabbi Lawrence Kushner*
5½ x 8½, 112 pp, Quality PB, 978-1-58023-150-3 **$12.95***

*A book from Jewish Lights, SkyLight Paths' sister imprint

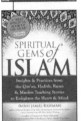

Women's Interest

She Lives! Sophia Wisdom Works in the World
By Rev. Jann Aldredge-Clanton, PhD
Fascinating narratives of clergy and laypeople who are changing the institutional church and society by restoring biblical female divine names and images to Christian theology, worship symbolism and liturgical language.
6 x 9, 320 pp, Quality PB, 978-1-59473-573-8 **$18.99**

Birthing God: Women's Experiences of the Divine
By Lana Dalberg; Foreword by Kathe Schaaf
Powerful narratives of suffering, love and hope that inspire both personal and collective transformation. 6 x 9, 304 pp, Quality PB, 978-1-59473-480-9 **$18.99**

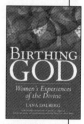

Women, Spirituality and Transformative Leadership
Where Grace Meets Power
Edited by Kathe Schaaf, Kay Lindahl, Kathleen S. Hurty, PhD, and Reverend Guo Cheen
A dynamic conversation on the power of women's spiritual leadership and its emerging patterns of transformation.
6 x 9, 288 pp, Quality PB, 978-1-59473-548-6 **$18.99**; HC, 978-1-59473-313-0 **$24.99**

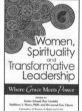

Spiritually Healthy Divorce: Navigating Disruption with Insight & Hope
By Carolyne Call A spiritual map to help you move through the twists and turns of divorce. 6 x 9, 224 pp, Quality PB, 978-1-59473-288-1 **$16.99**

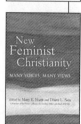

New Feminist Christianity: Many Voices, Many Views
Edited by Mary E. Hunt and Diann L. Neu
Insights from ministers and theologians, activists and leaders, artists and liturgists offer a starting point for building new models of religious life and worship.
6 x 9, 384 pp, Quality PB, 978-1-59473-435-9 **$19.99**; HC, 978-1-59473-285-0 **$24.99**

Bread, Body, Spirit: Finding the Sacred in Food
Edited and with Introductions by Alice Peck 6 x 9, 224 pp, Quality PB, 978-1-59473-242-3 **$19.99**

Dance—The Sacred Art: The Joy of Movement as a Spiritual Practice
By Cynthia Winton-Henry 5½ x 8½, 224 pp, Quality PB, 978-1-59473-268-3 **$16.99**

Daughters of the Desert: Stories of Remarkable Women from Christian, Jewish and Muslim Traditions
By Claire Rudolf Murphy, Meghan Nuttall Sayres, Mary Cronk Farrell, Sarah Conover and Betsy Wharton
5½ x 8½, 192 pp, Illus., Quality PB, 978-1-59473-106-8 **$14.99** Inc. reader's discussion guide

The Divine Feminine in Biblical Wisdom Literature
Selections Annotated & Explained
Translation & Annotation by Rabbi Rami Shapiro; Foreword by Rev. Cynthia Bourgeault, PhD
5½ x 8½, 240 pp, Quality PB, 978-1-59473-109-9 **$16.99**

Divining the Body: Reclaim the Holiness of Your Physical Self
By Jan Phillips 8 x 8, 256 pp, Quality PB, 978-1-59473-080-1 **$18.99**

Honoring Motherhood: Prayers, Ceremonies & Blessings
Edited and with Introductions by Lynn L. Caruso
5 x 7¼, 272 pp, Quality PB, 978-1-58473-384-0 **$9.99**; HC, 978-1-59473-239-3 **$19.99**

Next to Godliness: Finding the Sacred in Housekeeping
Edited by Alice Peck 6 x 9, 224 pp, Quality PB, 978-1-59473-214-0 **$19.99**

The Triumph of Eve & Other Subversive Bible Tales
By Matt Biers-Ariel 5½ x 8½, 192 pp, Quality PB, 978-1-59473-176-1 **$14.99**

Woman Spirit Awakening in Nature: Growing Into the Fullness of Who You Are
By Nancy Barrett Chickerneo, PhD; Foreword by Eileen Fisher
8 x 8, 224 pp, b/w illus., Quality PB, 978-1-59473-250-8 **$16.99**

Women of Color Pray: Voices of Strength, Faith, Healing, Hope and Courage
Edited and with Introductions by Christal M. Jackson
5 x 7¼, 208 pp, Quality PB, 978-1-59473-077-1 **$15.99**

*A book from Jewish Lights, SkyLight Paths' sister imprint

Spirituality

The Forgiveness Handbook
Spiritual Wisdom and Practice for the Journey to Freedom, Healing and Peace
By the Editors at SkyLight Paths

Offers inspiration, encouragement and spiritual practice from across faith traditions for all who seek hope, wholeness and the freedom that comes from true forgiveness.
6 x 9, 300 pp (est), Quality PB, 978-1-59473-577-6 **$18.99**

Like a Child
Restoring the Awe, Wonder, Joy and Resiliency of the Human Spirit
By Rev. Timothy J. Mooney

By breaking free from our misperceptions about what it means to be an adult, we can reshape our world and become harbingers of grace. This unique spiritual resource explores Jesus's counsel to become like children in order to enter the kingdom of God.   6 x 9, 160 pp, Quality PB, 978-1-59473-543-1 **$16.99**

The Passionate Jesus: What We Can Learn from Jesus about Love, Fear, Grief, Joy and Living Authentically
By The Rev. Peter Wallace

Reveals Jesus as a passionate figure who was involved, present, connected, honest and direct with others and encourages you to build personal authenticity in every area of your own life. 6 x 9, 208 pp, Quality PB, 978-1-59473-393-2 **$18.99**

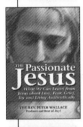

Gathering at God's Table: The Meaning of Mission in the Feast of Faith
By Katharine Jefferts Schori

A profound reminder of our role in the larger frame of God's dream for a restored and reconciled world.   6 x 9, 256 pp, HC, 978-1-59473-316-1 **$21.99**

The Heartbeat of God: Finding the Sacred in the Middle of Everything
By Katharine Jefferts Schori; Foreword by Joan Chittister, OSB

Explores our connections to other people, to other nations and with the environment through the lens of faith.
6 x 9, 240 pp, HC, 978-1-59473-292-8 **$21.99**

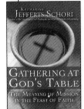

A Dangerous Dozen: Twelve Christians Who Threatened the Status Quo but Taught Us to Live Like Jesus
By the Rev. Canon C. K. Robertson, PhD; Foreword by Archbishop Desmond Tutu

Profiles twelve visionary men and women who challenged society and showed the world a different way of living.
6 x 9, 208 pp, Quality PB, 978-1-59473-298-0 **$16.99**

Laugh Your Way to Grace: Reclaiming the Spiritual Power of Humor
By Rev. Susan Sparks

A powerful, humorous case for laughter as a spiritual, healing path.
6 x 9, 176 pp, Quality PB, 978-1-59473-280-5 **$16.99**

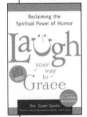

Claiming Earth as Common Ground: The Ecological Crisis through the Lens of Faith
By Andrea Cohen-Kiener; Foreword by Rev. Sally Bingham
6 x 9, 192 pp, Quality PB, 978-1-59473-261-4 **$16.99**

Living into Hope: A Call to Spiritual Action for Such a Time as This
By Rev. Dr. Joan Brown Campbell; Foreword by Karen Armstrong
6 x 9, 208 pp, Quality PB, 978-1-59473-436-6 $18.99; HC, 978-1-59473-283-6 **$21.99**

Renewal in the Wilderness:
A Spiritual Guide to Connecting with God in the Natural World
By John Lionberger 6 x 9, 176 pp, b/w photos, Quality PB, 978-1-59473-219-5 **$16.99**

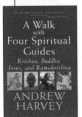

Spiritual Adventures in the Snow:
Skiing & Snowboarding as Renewal for Your Soul
By Dr. Marcia McFee and Rev. Karen Foster; Foreword by Paul Arthur
5½ x 8½, 208 pp, Quality PB, 978-1-59473-270-6 **$16.99**

A Walk with Four Spiritual Guides: Krishna, Buddha, Jesus, and Ramakrishna
By Andrew Harvey 5½ x 8½ 192 pp, b/w photos & illus., Quality PB, 978-1-59473-138-9 **$15.99**

Spirituality / Animal Companions

Blessing the Animals
Prayers and Ceremonies to Celebrate God's Creatures, Wild and Tame
Edited and with Introductions by Lynn L. Caruso
5 x 7¼, 256 pp, Quality PB, 978-1-59473-253-9 **$15.99**; HC, 978-1-59473-145-7 **$19.99**

Remembering My Pet
A Kid's Own Spiritual Workbook for When a Pet Dies
By Nechama Liss-Levinson, PhD, and Rev. Molly Phinney Baskette, MDiv
Foreword by Lynn L. Caruso
8 x 10, 48 pp, 2-color text, HC, 978-1-59473-221-8 **$16.99**

What Animals Can Teach Us about Spirituality
Inspiring Lessons from Wild and Tame Creatures
By Diana L. Guerrero 6 x 9, 176 pp, Quality PB, 978-1-893361-84-3 **$16.95**

Spirituality & Crafts

Beading—The Creative Spirit
Finding Your Sacred Center through the Art of Beadwork
By Rev. Wendy Ellsworth
Invites you on a spiritual pilgrimage into the kaleidoscope world of glass and color.
7 x 9, 240 pp, 8-page color insert, 40+ b/w photos and 40 diagrams, Quality PB, 978-1-59473-267-6 **$18.99**

Contemplative Crochet
A Hands-On Guide for Interlocking Faith and Craft
By Cindy Crandall-Frazier; Foreword by Linda Skolnik
Illuminates the spiritual lessons you can learn through crocheting.
7 x 9, 208 pp, b/w photos, Quality PB, 978-1-59473-238-6 **$16.99**

The Knitting Way
A Guide to Spiritual Self-Discovery
By Linda Skolnik and Janice MacDaniels
Examines how you can explore and strengthen your spiritual life through knitting.
7 x 9, 240 pp, b/w photos, Quality PB, 978-1-59473-079-5 **$16.99**

The Painting Path
Embodying Spiritual Discovery through Yoga, Brush and Color
By Linda Novick; Foreword by Richard Segalman
Explores the divine connection you can experience through art.
7 x 9, 208 pp, 8-page color insert, plus b/w photos, Quality PB, 978-1-59473-226-3 **$18.99**

The Quilting Path
A Guide to Spiritual Discovery through Fabric, Thread and Kabbalah
By Louise Silk
Explores how to cultivate personal growth through quilt making.
7 x 9, 192 pp, b/w photos and illus., Quality PB, 978-1-59473-206-5 **$16.99**

The Scrapbooking Journey
A Hands-On Guide to Spiritual Discovery
By Cory Richardson-Lauve; Foreword by Stacy Julian
Reveals how this craft can become a practice used to deepen and shape your life.
7 x 9, 176 pp, 8-page color insert, plus b/w photos, Quality PB, 978-1-59473-216-4 **$18.99**

The Soulwork of Clay
A Hands-On Approach to Spirituality
By Marjory Zoet Bankson; Photos by Peter Bankson
Takes you through the seven-step process of making clay into a pot, drawing parallels at each stage to the process of spiritual growth.
7 x 9, 192 pp, b/w photos, Quality PB, 978-1-59473-249-2 **$16.99**

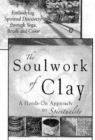

Spiritual Practice—The Sacred Art of Living Series

Dreaming—The Sacred Art: Incubating, Navigating & Interpreting Sacred Dreams for Spiritual & Personal Growth
By Lori Joan Swick
This fascinating introduction to sacred dreams celebrates the dream experience as a way to deepen spiritual awareness and as a source of self-healing. Designed for the novice and the experienced sacred dreamer of all faith traditions, or none.
5½ x 8½, 224 pp, Quality PB, 978-1-59473-544-8 **$16.99**

Conversation—The Sacred Art: Practicing Presence in an Age of Distraction
By Diane M. Millis, PhD; Foreword by Rev. Tilden Edwards, PhD
5½ x 8½, 192 pp, Quality PB, 978-1-59473-474-8 **$16.99**

Dance—The Sacred Art: The Joy of Movement as a Spiritual Practice
By Cynthia Winton-Henry 5½ x 8½, 224 pp, Quality PB, 978-1-59473-268-3 **$16.99**

Fly-Fishing—The Sacred Art: Casting a Fly as a Spiritual Practice
By Rabbi Eric Eisenkramer and Rev. Michael Attas, MD; Foreword by Chris Wood, CEO, Trout Unlimited; Preface by Lori Simon, executive director, Casting for Recovery
5½ x 8½, 160 pp, Quality PB, 978-1-59473-299-7 **$16.99**

Giving—The Sacred Art: Creating a Lifestyle of Generosity
By Lauren Tyler Wright 5½ x 8½, 208 pp, Quality PB, 978-1-59473-224-9 **$16.99**

Haiku—The Sacred Art: A Spiritual Practice in Three Lines
By Margaret D. McGee 5½ x 8½, 192 pp, Quality PB, 978-1-59473-269-0 **$16.99**

Hospitality—The Sacred Art: Discovering the Hidden Spiritual Power of Invitation and Welcome *By Rev. Nanette Sawyer; Foreword by Rev. Dirk Ficca*
5½ x 8½, 208 pp, Quality PB, 978-1-59473-228-7 **$16.99**

Labyrinths from the Outside In, 2nd Edition: Walking to Spiritual Insight—A Beginner's Guide *By Rev. Dr. Donna Schaper and Rev. Dr. Carole Ann Camp*
6 x 9, 208 pp, b/w illus. and photos, Quality PB, 978-1-59473-486-1 **$16.99**

Lectio Divina—**The Sacred Art**
Transforming Words & Images into Heart-Centered Prayer
By Christine Valters Paintner, PhD 5½ x 8½, 240 pp, Quality PB, 978-1-59473-300-0 **$16.99**

Pilgrimage—The Sacred Art: Journey to the Center of the Heart
By Dr. Sheryl A. Kujawa-Holbrook 5½ x 8½, 240 pp, Quality PB, 978-1-59473-472-4 **$16.99**

Practicing the Sacred Art of Listening: A Guide to Enrich Your Relationships and Kindle Your Spiritual Life *By Kay Lindahl* 8 x 8, 176 pp, Quality PB, 978-1-893361-85-0 **$18.99**

Recovery—The Sacred Art: The Twelve Steps as Spiritual Practice *by Rami Shapiro; Foreword by Joan Borysenko, PhD* 5½ x 8½, 240 pp, Quality PB, 978-1-59473-259-1 **$16.99**

Running—The Sacred Art: Preparing to Practice *By Dr. Warren A. Kay; Foreword by Kristin Armstrong* 5½ x 8½, 160 pp, Quality PB, 978-1-59473-227-0 **$16.99**

The Sacred Art of Chant: Preparing to Practice
By Ana Hernández 5½ x 8½, 192 pp, Quality PB, 978-1-59473-036-8 **$16.99**

The Sacred Art of Fasting: Preparing to Practice
By Thomas Ryan, CSP 5½ x 8½, 192 pp, Quality PB, 978-1-59473-078-8 **$15.99**

The Sacred Art of Forgiveness: Forgiving Ourselves and Others through God's Grace
By Marcia Ford 8 x 8, 176 pp, Quality PB, 978-1-59473-175-4 **$18.99**

The Sacred Art of Listening: Forty Reflections for Cultivating a Spiritual Practice
By Kay Lindahl; Illus. by Amy Schnapper 8 x 8, 160 pp, b/w illus., Quality PB, 978-1-893361-44-7 **$16.99**

The Sacred Art of Lovingkindness: Preparing to Practice
By Rabbi Rami Shapiro; Foreword by Marcia Ford 5½ x 8½, 176 pp, Quality PB, 978-1-59473-151-8 **$16.99**

Thanking & Blessing—The Sacred Art: Spiritual Vitality through Gratefulness
By Jay Marshall, PhD; Foreword by Philip Gulley 5½ x 8½, 176 pp, Quality PB, 978-1-59473-231-7 **$16.99**

Writing—The Sacred Art: Beyond the Page to Spiritual Practice
By Rami Shapiro and Aaron Shapiro 5½ x 8½, 192 pp, Quality PB, 978-1-59473-372-7 **$16.99**

Personal Growth

The Forgiveness Handbook
Spiritual Wisdom and Practice for the Journey to Freedom, Healing and Peace
By the Editors at SkyLight Paths
Offers inspiration, encouragement and spiritual practice from across faith traditions for all who seek hope, wholeness and the freedom that comes from true forgiveness.   6 x 9, 300 pp (est), Quality PB, 978-1-59473-577-6 **$18.99**

Decision Making & Spiritual Discernment: The Sacred Art of
Finding Your Way *By Nancy L. Bieber*
Presents three essential aspects of Spirit-led decision making: willingness, attentiveness and responsiveness.
5½ x 8½, 208 pp, Quality PB, 978-1-59473-289-8 **$16.99**

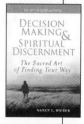

Like a Child
Restoring the Awe, Wonder, Joy and Resiliency of the Human Spirit
By Rev. Timothy J. Mooney
Explores Jesus's counsel to become like children in order to enter the kingdom of God.   6 x 9, 160 pp, Quality PB, 978-1-59473-543-1 **$16.99**

Secrets of a Soulful Marriage
Creating & Sustaining a Loving, Sacred Relationship
By Jim Sharon, EdD, and Ruth Sharon, MS
An innovative, hope-filled resource for developing soulful, mature love for committed couples who are looking to create, maintain and glorify the sacred in their relationship. Offers a banquet of practical tools, inspirational real-life stories and spiritual practices for couples of all faiths, or none.
6 x 9, 192 pp, Quality PB, 978-1-59473-554-7 **$16.99**

Conversation—The Sacred Art
Practicing Presence in an Age of Distraction
By Diane M. Millis, PhD; Foreword by Rev. Tilden Edwards, PhD
5½ x 8½, 192 pp, Quality PB, 978-1-59473-474-8 **$16.99**

Hospitality—The Sacred Art
Discovering the Hidden Spiritual Power of Invitation and Welcome
By Rev. Nanette Sawyer; Foreword by Rev. Dirk Ficca
Discover how the qualities of hospitality can deepen your self-understanding and help you build transforming and lasting relationships with others and with God.
5½ x 8½, 208 pp, Quality PB, 978-1-59473-228-7 **$16.99**

The Losses of Our Lives
The Sacred Gifts of Renewal in Everyday Loss
By Dr. Nancy Copeland-Payton
Shows us that by becoming aware of what our lesser losses have to teach us, the larger losses become less terrifying. Includes spiritual practices and questions for reflection.
6 x 9, 192 pp, Quality PB, 978-1-59473-307-9 **$16.99**; HC, 978-1-59473-271-3 **$19.99**

A Spirituality for Brokenness
Discovering Your Deepest Self in Difficult Times
By Terry Taylor
Compassionately guides you through the practicalities of facing and finally accepting brokenness in your life—a process that can ultimately bring mending.
6 x 9, 176 pp, Quality PB, 978-1-59473-229-4 **$16.99**

The Bridge to Forgiveness
Stories and Prayers for Finding God and Restoring Wholeness
By Karyn D. Kedar
Inspiring, deeply personal stories, comforting prayers and intimate meditations gently lead you through the steps that allow the heart to forgive.
6 x 9, 176 pp, Quality PB, 978-1-58023-451-1 **$16.99***

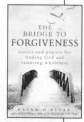

*A book from Jewish Lights, SkyLight Paths' sister imprint

About SKYLIGHT PATHS Publishing

SkyLight Paths Publishing is creating a place where people of different spiritual traditions come together for challenge and inspiration, a place where we can help each other understand the mystery that lies at the heart of our existence.

Through spirituality, our religious beliefs are increasingly becoming a part of our lives—rather than *apart* from our lives. While many of us may be more interested than ever in spiritual growth, we may be less firmly planted in traditional religion. Yet, we do want to deepen our relationship to the sacred, to learn from our own as well as from other faith traditions, and to practice in new ways.

SkyLight Paths sees both believers and seekers as a community that increasingly transcends traditional boundaries of religion and denomination—people wanting to learn from each other, *walking together, finding the way.*

For your information and convenience, at the back of this book we have provided a list of other SkyLight Paths books you might find interesting and useful. They cover the following subjects:

Buddhism / Zen	Gnosticism	Poetry
Catholicism	Hinduism / Vedanta	Prayer
Chaplaincy		Religious Etiquette
Children's Books	Inspiration	Retirement & Later-Life Spirituality
Christianity	Islam / Sufism	
Comparative Religion	Judaism	Spiritual Biography
	Meditation	Spiritual Direction
Earth-Based Spirituality	Mindfulness	Spirituality
	Monasticism	Women's Interest
Enneagram	Mysticism	Worship
Global Spiritual Perspectives	Personal Growth	

Or phone, fax, mail or email to: SKYLIGHT PATHS Publishing
Sunset Farm Offices, Route 4 • P.O. Box 237 • Woodstock, Vermont 05091
Tel: (802) 457-4000 • Fax: (802) 457-4004 • www.skylightpaths.com
Credit card orders: (800) 962-4544 (8:30AM–5:30PM EST Monday–Friday)
Generous discounts on quantity orders. SATISFACTION GUARANTEED. Prices subject to change.

**For more information about each book,
visit our website at www.skylightpaths.com**